Puja

The Process of Ritualistic Worship

MATA AMRITANANDAMAYI MISSION TRUST
AMRITAPURI, KERALA, INDIA

When everything is set perfectly, the pujari closes his eyes and sits quietly for a brief moment, tuning his mind to the Lord and the sacred puja he is about to perform. He sits before the shrine cross-legged. He can sit either facing the Lord or facing north. The Lord should face east or north. The pujari should not block the view of the altar from the persons attending. Throughout the worship, all offerings are made with the right hand only although there are occasions when both hands are used. While offering the various items, the left hand is held touching the right elbow in order to complete the "circuit" of the nervous system, thus making the offering "full".

The offering of food is an important part of puja. Fresh fruits should be offered. The food is kept covered until the food offering section of the puja is reached. The food is then uncovered and offered to the Deity. The Deity can partake of the subtle essence of the food. Keeping the food covered until making the offering helps to preserve its purity by not allowing anyone to gaze upon it. After the puja, the food may be enjoyed by the devotees as *prasadam,* that which has been offered to and blessed by the Deity.

Offering a spoon of water to the Deity means that one takes a spoon of water with the left hand and, holding a flower in the right hand, one pours the water into the right hand and then offers that water into the plate with that hand. The lighted lamp should not face south or west. Hands must be washed with a spoonful of water if they come into contact with sources of impurity, i.e. the lamp, things already offered to the Deity, one's own feet, legs, head, mouth, lips, nose, hair, or the ground. These rules are intended to keep you alert. Yawning, sneezing and coughing create impurity. If unavoidable, keep your hand and tissue before your mouth. Afterwards, touch your right ear three times, repeating the Divine Name for purification. Smelling, tasting or enjoying things to be offered to the Deity is strictly prohibited. After the puja, it is permissable to enjoy them as *prasadam*.

The following articles should not touch the ground or carpet but should have a leaf or plate put under them if unavoidable: the Deity, bell, water vessel, lamp, flowers, clothes of the Deity, water (sacred water), prasad, camphor. If flowers are not available, leaves of flower trees, basil leaves, rice or kumkum can be used as a substitute. Steel, plastic and iron vessels may not be used. After puja, dispose of the offered flowers, water, etc. at the foot of a tree or in a river or some place where no will will step on them.

In the beginning of the puja, the pujari recites a section called the *Sankalpa,* the intention of the ritual. Once this is recited, he may not stop the puja, fail to complete it or respond to other duties. If time does not permit, the puja can be done in an abbreviated form offering only bath, light, incense, food and flowers followed by arati. Even if hurried, the puja is not complete until the concluding mantra is spoken. After the puja,the pujari may sit and enjoy the resultant peace or meditate for a while.

This puja has been designed having in mind Mata Amritanandamayi as the Deity, as She is the usual object of worship for Her devotees. Mother's devotees will no doubt be doing their puja in order to gain Her Grace, as Guru's Grace is the ultimate blessing for a disciple or devotee of a Realized Soul. However, sets of 108 Names have been included at the end of the book for Devi, Krishna, Rama and Shiva. The process of puja is basically the same for any aspect of God. A few places in the *Sankalpa* section have been marked which should be changed according to the aspect of God being worshipped. The *mula* (basic) *mantra* for the puja is OM AMṚTEŚVARYE NAMAḤ which is to be repeated before each offering. One can use either the English or the Sanskrit verses or both, as per ease of use. The various materials and vessels for puja can be obtained from the many shops around the country catering to the Indian (from India) community. A pronunciation key is at the end of this book.

Suddhi

PURIFICATION

The first stage of worship consists of purification by driving out the "demonic forces" or bad tendencies and invoking devas or good tendencies.

Ātma Śudhi (Self-purification)

After sitting on an asana or seat, the pujari should take a spoonful of water from his water pot and wash his right hand into the waste water plate in order to ritually cleanse it. He should then pour another spoonful of water into the right hand and say:

ACYUTÀYA NAMAÃ	Salutations to the Immovable
ANANTÀYA NAMAÃ	Salutations to the Infinite
GOVINDÀYA NAMAÃ	Salutations to Lord of the senses

sipping one spoonful of water from the heel of the right hand with the repetition of each name. Finally, the right hand should be washed with a spoon of water into the waste plate. This sipping of water is called *achamanam* or purificatory sipping. Three pranayamas should be done

after this. Hold the right hand as in the photo and press the thumb against the right nostril while inhaling through the left nostril. Retain the breath for about two seconds and then closing the left nostril with the last two fingers, exhale through the right nostril. Now inhale through the right nostril while keeping the left nostril closed with the last two fingers. Retain the breath for two seconds and then exhale through the left nostril while closing the right nostril. This is counted as one pranayama. While doing this, imagine that one is inhaling divine, purifying life force or *prana shakti*, and while exhaling, one is expelling all thoughts except the thought of God.

Āsana Śuddhi - Purification of the seat

Sprinkle a few drops of water held in the right hand on your seat or àsana and say:

> ***O Mother Earth, you carry everything in Creation on your lap, and you are holy because the Supreme Lord supports you. Because of my sitting on you, kindly sanctify me and this seat.***

Deepa Puja

WORSHIP OF THE LAMP

Light the secondary lamp and with that, light the main lamp. Daub a bit of sandalwood paste and kumkum on the head and base of the lamp and offer a flower at the foot of the lamp saying:

> ***Salutations to the Light of lights! May you dispel the darkness of ignorance and bestow upon me steadiness of mind.***
>
> OM DĪPA PUJA SAMARPAYĀMI

Ghanta Puja

WORSHIP OF THE BELL

Daub sandalwood paste and kumkum on the forehead of the bell, offer flowers at its base and say:

> ***Salutations to all of the devas (gods)! Let the sound of this bell, OM, vibrate in my heart. May all the good tendencies, the devas, be invoked in my heart, and let all evil vibrations cease to be.***

OM ĀVĀHITĀBHYO SARVĀBHYO
DEVATĀBHYO NAMAḤ

Ring the bell loudly with the right hand and say,

GHANTA PUJA SAMARPAYĀMI

Kalasa Puja

INVOKING THE HOLY WATERS

Daub sandalwood paste and kumkum on three sides of the pot containing sacred water and put flowers and holy leaves, sandalwood paste and rice in the pot and holding the right hand on the mouth of the pot, pray:

May Lord Vishnu be invoked in the mouth of the pot, Lord Rudra in the throat, Lord Brahma in the base and the Mothers of the World in the middle portion.

KALAŚASYE MUKHE VIṢṆUḤ
KAṆṬHE RUDRAḤ SAMĀŚRITAḤ
MŪLE TATRA STHITO BRAHMĀ
MADHYE MĀTṚGAṆĀ SMṚTĀḤ

O Rivers Ganga, Yamuna, Godavari, Saraswati, Narmada, Sindhu and Kaveri - please be present in this holy water. May all the sacred rivers of the world be present here.

GANGE CHĀ YAMUNE CHAIVĀ GODĀVARĪ SARASVATI
NARMADE SINDHŪ KĀVERI
JALESMIN SANNIDHIM KURU

Dip a flower in the holy water and sprinkle some water on the Deity, on oneself, and on the puja things using the flower.

Sankalpa

RESOLVE

Pour a spoon of water and a pinch of rice and a flower or a tulasi leaf in the right hand and put the left palm over the right palm, resting both on the right knee while reciting the *Sankalpa*. Depending on the hour of day that the puja is performed, one of the times of day shown on the next page is inserted in the place indicated for it. After the chanting , the rice and water is poured into the plate that is used for bathing the Deity as the last word, *Karisye,* is spoken. Once the *Sankalpa* is said, the puja may not be interrupted or left off by the pujari before the concluding mantras are recited.

Now, at this auspicious moment, in the time of Eternity, in the place of Omnipresence, on this auspicious day, may I please You, O Satguru Amritanandamayi Devi. That I may attain devotion, wisdom and dispassion, I undertake to perform this worship of the Supreme Goddess (or Deity being worshipped).

OṀ ĀDYA EVAM GUṆA SAKALĀ
VIŚEṢENA VIŚIṢṬĀYĀM
ASYĀM ŚUBHATITHAU
OṀ MĀTĀ AMṚTĀNANDAMAYI DEVIM UDDIŚYA
SATGURU PRĪTYĀRTHAM
BHAKTI JÑĀNA VAIRĀGYA SIDDHYĀRTHAM
YATHĀ ŚAKTĪ (insert the time of day)*
PARAMEŚVARĪ (or deity being worshipped)
PŪJANAM KARĪŚYE

*uṣat kāla = pre-dawn
prātaḥ kāla = sunrise
madhyāna kāla = daytime
sāyam kāla = evening
śayana kāla = nighttime

Vigneshwara Puja

Recall to mind Lord Ganesh's form, or, if there is an image of Ganesh, daub some sandalwood paste and kumkum on Him, place a flower at His feet, and raising the hands with palms joined, say:

OM. O Lord Ganesh dressed in splendid white, pervading all the universe, shining radiantly like the ivory rays of the full moon, having four mighty arms and a charming, happy face, I meditate on You thus, Lord, that all obstacles may be quelled and made peaceful.

OṀ ŚUKLĀMBARADHARAM VIṢNUM
ŚAŚIVARṆAM CATURBHUJAM
PRASANNA VADANAM DHYĀYET
SARVA VIGHNOPA ŚĀNTAYE
ŚRĪ GANEṢA PRĀRTHANA SAMĀRPAYĀMI

ॐ Atma Puja

Put sacred ash and kumkum (optional) on one's own forehead and pray:

OṀ ĀTMANE NAMAḤ	O Self! Salutations.
OṀ ANTARĀTMANE NAMAḤ	O Inner Self! Salutations.
OṀ PARAMĀTMANE NAMAḤ	O Supreme Self! Salutations.
OṀ JÑĀNĀTMANE NAMAḤ	O Self of Knowledge! Salutations.

Then place a flower on your own head, remembering that Mother resides in your own heart as the 'I' shining within you and say,

ĀTMA PŪJA SAMARPAYĀMI

Dhyanam

MEDITATION

Hold the hands with palms joined and visualizing Mother sitting in front of you, pray:

I meditate on Mata Amritanandamayi whose head is covered with a white garment, who is effulgent, who is ever-established in Truth, whose glances beam with binding love, who is the Source of godly qualities, whose radiant smile adorns Her face with auspiciousness, who incessantly showers the nectar of affection, who sings devotional songs most sweetly, whose complexion resembles that of the rainclouds, whose words are soaked in honey, who is Bliss Immortal and who is the Supreme Goddess Herself.

DHYĀYĀMO–DHAVALĀVAGUṆṬHANA–VATĪṀ
TEJOMAYĪM–NAIṢṬHIKĪṀ
SNIGDHĀPĀṄGA–VILOKINĪM–BHAGAVATĪṀ
MANDASMITA–ŚRĪ–MUKHĪṀ
VĀTSALYĀMṚTA–VARṢIṆĪM–SU–MADHURAṀ
SAṀ–KĪṚTTANĀLĀPINĪṀ
ŚYĀMĀṄGĪṀ–MADHU–SIKTA–SŪKTĪṀ
AMṚTĀNANDĀTMIKĀMĪŚVARĪṀ

Offer a flower to Mother and say:

O Satguru Mata Amritanandamayi, please accept this meditation!

OṀ AMṚTEŚVARYE NAMAḤ
SATGURU MĀTĀ AMṚTĀNANDAMAYĪM DHYĀYĀMI

Sthana Peeta Puja

WORSHIP OF THE DEITY'S SEAT

Put kumkum in the center of the plate for bathing the Deity and chant "OM" three times.

Avahanam

INVITATION

Take a flower and hold it against the heart. Imagine that Mother is residing in your heart. Take a deep breath and slowly breathe out through the nostrils on to the flower, imagining that Mother's Presence has entered the flower. Then touch the flower to Mother's head and pass it down to the feet. Put flowers on the bathing plate. Hold the palms facing up and showing the plate to Mother, invite Her to sit there saying,

O Mother, omniscient, omnipresent One, please grace this puja and come and sit firmly in my mind, blessing me with Your Presence and proximity. Welcome, welcome to You!

OṀ AMṚTEŚVARYE NAMAḤ
SATGURU MĀTĀ AMṚTĀNANDAMAYĪM ĀVĀHAYĀMI

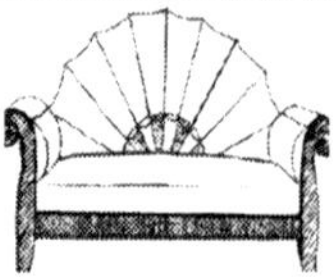

Asanam

SEAT

Visualize Mother seated on a golden throne before you, smiling, full of blessings, and waiting to be honored as a guest. Offering a flower at Her feet, say,

In all splendor I have prepared for You a Jewel-studded, lion-footed throne to sit upon, O Mother. Abiding in my heart and bestowing everlasting joy, kindly accept this offering!

OṀ AMṚTEŚVARYE NAMAḤ
RATNA SIṀHĀSANAM SAMARPAYĀMI

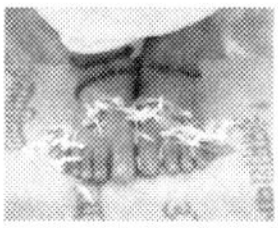

Padyam & Arghyam

WASHING THE FEET AND HANDS

Pour a spoonful of holy water into your right hand along with a flower and offer it to Mother by holding it up before Her momentarily and then placing it in the bathing plate. This is how all water offering is done throughout the puja. As you speak these lines, visualize washing Mother's feet. Again offer a spoonful of pure water as you speak the second line, visualizing washing Her hands.

I now humbly bathe each of Your lotus feet which are the source of the holy rivers, the object of meditation of yogis, and the support of helpless devotees. I gently wash each of Your precious hands, which are engaged in uplifting Dharma, comforting devotees and putting off obstacles in the path of Liberation, O Mother, the Protector of Dharma and Bestower of Prosperity and Liberation.

OṀ AMṚTEŚVARYE NAMAḤ
PĀDAYOḤ PĀDYAM SAMARPAYĀMI
HASTAYOḤ ARGHYAM SAMARPAYĀMI

Achamaniyam

PURIFICATORY SIPPING

Offer a spoonful of water to Mother, visualizing that She is taking it in Her hand to sip, and say,

O Mother, I humbly offer You fresh, pure water for sipping.

OṀ AMṚTEŚVARYE NAMAḤ
ĀCAMANAM SAMARPAYĀMI

Madhuparkam

HONEY AND YOGURT

Offer a spoonful of yogurt and a bit of honey as a refreshment to Mother and say,

O Mother, please accept this offering of honeyed curd.

OṀ AMṚTEŚVARYE NAMAḤ
MADHUPARKAM SAMARPAYĀMI

Abhishekam

BATH

Remove the dress primarily with your right hand and put on a separate plate. Used dress should be washed in fresh water after puja and dried for the next time Take a few drops of oil in the right palm and touch the head of the Deity. Then annoint the whole body with it. Of course, if a photo is being used as the Deity, oil, water and similar materials should not be put on it. They should just be shown to the photo and then offered into the bathing plate. While ringing the bell, continuously repeat:

OṀ AMṚTEŚVARYE NAMAḤ

while pouring water over the Deity using the spoon. If possible, the following items can also be used for bathing, pouring water over the Deity between each item:

1) milk
2) yogurt (curd)
3) honey
4) ghee
5) fruit salad
6) coconut water (the milk of the coconut)
7) rosewater

Finally, bathe Mother with pure water and say,

O Mother, may You accept this bath with the pure and clean water from the holy rivers Ganga, Godavari, Krishna and Yamuna who have all come here.

GAṄGĀ GODĀVARĪ KṚṢṆĀ YAMUNĀBHYAḤ
SAMĀHṚTAM
SALILAṀ VIMALAṀ ŚUDDHAṀ SNĀNĀRTHA
PRATIGṚHṚTĀM
OṀ AMṚTEŚVARYE NAMAḤ
ŚUDDHODAKENA SNAPAYĀMI

After bathing the Deity, offer a spoonful of water and say,

Kindly accept this cool water for sipping after Your bath.

SNĀNĀNANTARAM ĀCAMANĪYAM SAMARPAYĀMI

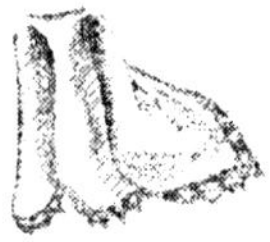

Vastram

DRESS

Dry the Deity with a clean cloth and place Her on a dry plate or silk cloth on the altar. Drape a fresh piece of cloth or dress on Her or offer a flower or a pinch of rice, and say,

O Mother, all-pervading One, please accept this resplendent clothing

OṀ AMṚTEŚVARYE NAMAḤ
VASTRAM SAMARPAYĀMI

Upaveetam

SACRED THREAD

Offer a sacred thread or a flower or rice and say,

O Mother, Bestower of the fruit of actions, please accept this white cotton thread of divine action.

OṀ AMṚTEŚVARYE NAMAḤ
UPAVĪTAM SAMARPAYĀMI

Abharanam

ORNAMENTS

Decorate Mother with ornaments or offer a flower or rice and say,

Mock me not who seeks Your protection; ornament me with Your Grace and save me, O Mother! Please accept this offering of ornaments.

OṀ AMṚTEŚVARYE NAMAḤ
ĀBHARAṆAM SAMARPAYĀMI

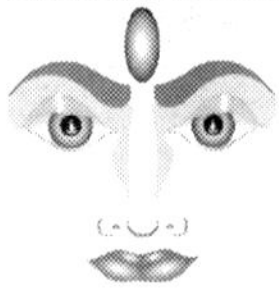

Chandanam

SANDALWOOD PASTE, KUMKUM AND VIBHUTI

Put a bit of sacred ash, sandalwood paste and kumkum on the forehead of the Deity using one's ring finger and say,

May this divine fragrance be the means to open the doors of nourishment and well-being. May they flood out in never-ending supply, O Mother of all living creatures. As one lost in the dark would call for light, I call upon You. Now I anoint You with pure, white sacred ash, fragrant sandalwood paste and red kumkum.

GANDHADVĀRAM DURADHARṢAM
NITYA PUṢṬAM KARĪṢINĪṀ
ĪŚVARĪGAM SARVA BHŪTĀNĀM
TĀMIHOPAHVAYE ṢRĪYAM
OṀ AMṚTEŚVARYE NAMAḤ
DIVYA PARIMĀLĀ VIBHŪTĪ
KUMKUMA CANDANAM DHĀRAYĀMI

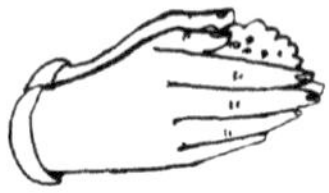

Pushpam

FLOWERS

Offer a handful of flowers and say,

For the fulfillment of my devotion to You, I offer fresh blooming flowers for Your enjoyment, O peerless Mother!

OṀ AMṚTEŚVARYE NAMAḤ
PŪJĀRTHE NĀNĀ VIDHA PATRA PUṢPĀNI PŪJAYĀMI

Archana

108 (OR 1000) NAMES OF THE DEITY

Repeat the 108 or 1000 names of the Deity, offering a flower or a piece of rice or kumkum with each name, hlolding it to your heart and then, having the palm face upward, dropping it on the Deity's feet or head after saying the name. The forefinger should not be used. (See the various sets of 108 Names at the end of this book)

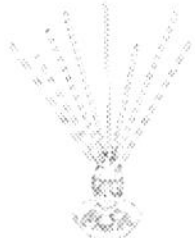

Dhupam

INCENSE

Light at least 2 sticks of incense from the secondary lamp and offer the smoke to the Deity waving the sticks clockwise three times in front of the Deity's face while ringing the bell. Say,

> ***I offer this fine incense of varied fragrance for Your pleasure to be inhaled and enjoyed by You.***

OṀ AMṚTEŚVARYE NAMAḤ
DHŪPAM AGHRĀPAYĀMI

Deepam

LIGHT

Light the deepam spoon from the secondary lamp, daub a bit of sandalwood paste and kumkum on it, and holding a flower with it in your right hand, wave it clockwise before the Deity three times while ringing the bell. After setting it down, say,

> ***I have set blazing this auspicious light before You. For within fire is spiritual knowledge, because of which no harm can befall me. O Mother, may purity and peace spread all around me, as this holy flame illumines all with clarity!***

OṀ AMṚTEŚVARYE NAMAḤ
DIVYA MAṄGALA DĪPAM SANDARŚAYĀMI

Please accept this divine flame, O Light of lights!

Offer a spoonful of water for purificatory sipping, saying,

This incense and flame have been duly offered to You. Now once again accept this cool, sweet water for sipping.

OṀ AMṚTEŚVARYE NAMAḤ
DŪPA DĪPĀNANTARAM ĀCAMANĪYAM SAMARPAYĀMI

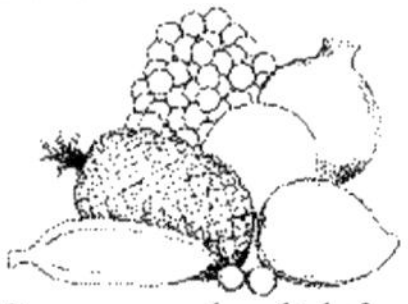

Naivedyam

FOOD

Remove the lid from the food offering. Holding a flower in the right hand, dip the flower into the holy water and sprinkle some water on the food. Then, pour a spoon of water into your right hand and make a circle around the offering three times, allowing the water to slowly flow out between your fingers onto the altar around the food offering. Then offer the food to the Deity by sweeping the right hand over the food and up to the mouth of the Deity six times, repeating the following, one line for each sweep:

OṀ PRĀṆĀYA SVĀHĀ
OṀ APĀNĀYA SVĀHĀ
OṀ VYĀNĀYA SVĀHĀ
OṀ UDĀNĀYA SVĀHĀ
OṀ SAMĀNĀYA SVĀHĀ
OṀ BRAHMAṆE SVĀHĀ

I offer You the five vital pranas in this food which sustain life. In all sincerity and love, I offer You the essence of this humble plate of food. May You receive it and count it as among the finest of meals, O Mother.

OṀ AMṚTEŚVARYE NAMAḤ
NĀNĀ VIDHA MAHĀ NAIVEDYAM NIVEDAYĀMI

One should then offer Mother five spoons of water, one after the other, saying,

During Your meal I now bring You cool water to drink, and the same to conclude Your meal. Here now is water for rinsing Your hands and Your mouth, O Mother, and more cool sweet water for sipping.

MADHYE MADHYE SĪTALA PĀNĪYAM SAMARPAYĀMI
UTTARĀPOṢANAM SAMARPAYĀMI
HASTA PRAKṢĀLANAM SAMARPAYĀMI
MUKHA PRAKṢĀLANAM SAMARPAYĀMI
ŚUDDHĀCAMANĪYAM SAMARPAYĀMI

Tambulam

BETEL LEAVES AND NUTS

Offering a flower or rice or tambulam if available, say,

I offer fresh betel leaf and lime for Your enjoyment, O Mother.

OṀ AMṚTEŚVARYE NAMAḤ
TĀṀBŪLAM SAMARPAYĀMI

Karpura Nirajanam

CAMPHOR FLAME

Light the spoon of camphor, daub some sandalpaste and kumkum on it, and holding a flower on it, wave it clockwise three times before the Deity, starting at the feet, while repeating the following and ringing the bell:

OṀ JAYA JAYA JAGAJANANĪ VANDE
AMṚTĀNANDAMAYĪ
MAṄGALA ĀRATI MĀTĀ BHAVĀNĪ AMṚTĀNANDAMAYĪ
MĀTĀ AMṚTĀNANDAMAYĪ MĀTĀ AMṚTĀNANDAMAYĪ
OṀ AMṚTEŚVARYE NAMAḤ
DIVYA MAṄGALA NIRĀJANAM DARŚAYĀMI

Victory to the Mother of the Universe, Amritanandamayi, obeisance to You. Most auspicious and divine arati to You, Mother Bhavani.

Offer a spoonful of water to the Deity and say,

O Mother, please accept this cool sweet water for sipping.

OṀ AMṚTEŚVARYE NAMAḤ
ĀCAMANĪYAM SAMARPAYĀMI

After concluding this mantra, the pujari passes the flame to the others present, who partake of it by three times waving the fingers of both hands through it and lightly touching the eyes with the fingers each time as the flame is held before them. The fingers should pass through the flame. The pujari carries the flame clockwise around the room, taking care to pass it first to any especially honorable persons that may be present, such as one's Guru, parents or teacher. If no one is present in the shrine room, then the pujari may take the flame himself, otherwise he does not. The flame must be presented once more to the murthis on the altar before it is extinguished with a wave of the right hand. This extinguishing of the flame is never done directly in front of the altar. The pujari would generally turn to his left and extinguish the flame out of the view of those attending.

Mantra Pushpam

FLOWERS WITH PRAISES

Hold fresh flowers in your cupped palms in front of you in salutation. The hands are cupped loosely around the flowers. If no flowers are available, rice may be offered. The verses are recited with devotion, and as the last word *samarpayami is* spoken, the flowers are thrown into the air slightly above the altar, thus creating a shower of blossoms upon the Deity.

I hasten with fresh, blooming flowers to adore the Mother of the Universe. O Mother, be pleased with this offering of fresh flowers representing my heart lotus.

OṀ AMṚTEŚVARYE NAMAḤ
MANTRAPUṢPĀṆI SAMARPAYĀMI

Atmapradakshina Namaskaram

CIRCUMAMBULATION AND PROSTRATION

Turn around clockwise in a circle three times in front of the altar, and then prostrate before the Deity and after getting up, say,

O all-pervading Divine Mother, be gracious and accept this my pranam.

OṀ AMṚTEŚVARYE NAMAḤ
ĀTMA PRADAKṢINA NAMASKĀRAM SAMARPAYĀMI

Nrityam & Geetam

DANCE AND SONG

Dance before the Deity or offer a flower and say,

O Mother, be pleased with my dance.

OṀ AMṚTEŚVARYE NAMAḤ
NṚTYAM DARŚAYĀMI

Sing a bhajan or hymn and then say,

OṀ AMṚTEŚVARYE NAMAḤ
GĪTAM SRAVAYĀMI

May You be pleased listening to my praises of You.

Offer a flower for each of the following items saying,

O Mother, accept this offering of an umbrella, chamara (yak-tail fan), fan, mirror and all other royal paraphernalia.

OṀ AMṚTEŚVARYE NAMAḤ
CHATRA CĀMARA VYAJANA DARPAṆĀDI
SAMASTA RĀJOPACĀRĀN SAMARPAYĀMI

Consecration & Surrender

Before reciting the following verse, take a pinch of rice in the right fingers, place it in the left palm, then immediately transfer it to the right palm. To this rice in the right palm is added three spoonfuls of pure water. This mixture is held up before the Deity, the left hand under the right hand, and the verse is recited. As the last words are spoken, the mixture is allowed to fall into the plate. This verse represents the ritual conclusion of the puja. Up to this point, the pujari may not leave off the ceremony nor leave the shrine area. The sacraments (prasadam) may now be passed around in the following order: sacred ash, sandalwood, kumkum, flowers, tirtham (holy water) and naivedyam. After everyone has partaken of the prasadam, the pujari may partake of them himself.

Now to the best of my ability I have performed this puja and worshipped You, dear Mother, the brightest of all the gods. May it please You, may it be enjoyed by You. Surrounded by Your presence, I place myself in Your care, O Mother.

ANENA YATHĀ ŚAKTYĀ KṚTA
(state time of day - see Sankalpa section)
PŪJAYĀ BHAGAVATĪ SARVA DEVATĀMIKA
ŚRĪ AMṚTEŚVARI SUPRĪTA
SUPRASANNA VARADA BHAVATU

Pardoning

This concluding apology is recited with hands in namaskaram, and typically the pujari will prostrate before the altar at the completion of the verse. It is the formal and devout end to the worship.

O Supreme Goddess, I know not the proper means of invoking You or communicating with You as You are. A full knowledge of priestly rites has not been imparted, so kindly overlook and forgive any mistakes or omissions. I know little of mantras or pious conduct, and I am a stranger to true devotion. Nonetheless for give me, and whatsoever worship I have been able to do, accept it as full and complete because You are my only refuge, my Supreme Empress. For me there is no other. Because of this have mercy, O Mother, and protect me who prays to You.

OṀ ĀVĀHANAM NA JĀNĀMI NA JĀNĀMI VISARJANAM
PŪJĀÑCAIVA NA JĀNĀMI KṢAMYATĀM PARAMEŚVARĪ
MANTRA HĪNAM KRIYĀ HĪNAM
BHAKTI HĪNAM SUREŚVARĪ
YATPŪJITAM MAYĀ DEVI
PARIPŪRṆAM TADASTU TE
ANYATHĀ ŚARAṆAM NĀSTI
TVAMEVA ŚARAṆAM MAMA
TASMĀT KĀRUṆYA BHĀVENA
RAKṢA RAKṢA MAHEŚVARĪ

Take a flower from the Deity's feet. Smell it and touch it to your heart imagining that the Lord's Presence which had been invoked into the image from your heart at the beginning of the puja has once again been placed back into the heart. Say,

OṀ AMṚTEŚVARYE NAMAḤ
ASMĀT KANDĀT ASMĀT BIMBĀT
YATHĀ STHĀNAṀ PRATIṢṬHĀPAYĀMI
ŚOBHANĀRTHE KṢEMĀYA PUNARĀGAMANĀYA CA

O Mother, please return to Your Abode, my heart, and bless me again in future with Your Presence for my betterment and liberation.

OṀ TAT SAT

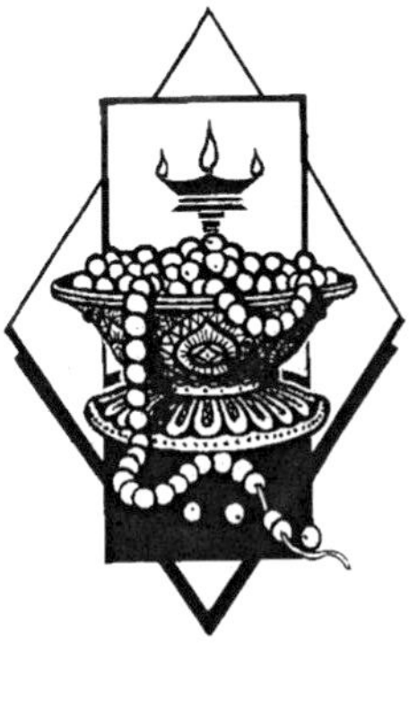

108 Names of Mata Amritanandamayi

OṀ PŪṚṆA–BRAHMA–SVARŪPIṆYAI NAMAḤ

Salutations to Her who is the complete manifestation of the absolute Truth (Brahman).

OṀ SACCIDĀNANDA–MŪRTAYE NAMAḤ

...who is existence, knowledge and bliss embodied.

OṀ ĀTMĀ–RĀMĀGRAGAṆYĀYAI NAMAḤ

...who is supreme among those who revel in the inner Self.

OṀ YOGA–LĪNĀNTARĀTMANE NAMAḤ

...whose inner Self (pure mind) is merged in Yoga (the union of the individual Self and Brahman).

OṀ ANTAR–MUKHA–SVABHĀVĀYAI NAMAḤ

...whose very nature is inwardly drawn.

OṀ TURYA–TUṄGA–STHALĪJUṢE NAMAḤ

...who dwells in the top-most plane of consciousness known as 'turiya'.

OṀ PṚABHĀ–MAṆḌALA–VĪTĀYAI NAMAḤ

...who is totally surrounded by divine light.

OṀ DURĀSADA–MAHAUJASE NAMAḤ

...whose greatness is unsurpassable.

OṀ TYAKTA–DIG–VASTU–KĀLĀDI–SAṚVĀVACCEDA–RĀŚAYE NAMAḤ

...who has risen above all the limitations of space, matter and time.

OṀ SAJĀTĪYA–VIJĀTĪYA–SVĪYA–BHEDA–NIRĀKṚTE NAMAḤ

...who is devoid of all kinds of differences ('differences' as usually seen among the same species, between different species, and within one and the same individual).

OṀ VĀṆĪ–BUDDHI–VIMṚGYĀYAI NAMAḤ

...whom speech and intellect cannot apprehend.

OṀ ŚAŚVAD–AVYAKTA–VARTMANE NAMAḤ

...whose path is eternally non-defined.

OṀ NĀMA–RŪPĀDI–ŚŪNYĀYAI NAMAḤ

...who is devoid of name and form.

OṀ ŚŪNYA–KALPA–VIBHŪTAYE NAMAḤ

...to whom the yogic powers are of no importance (like the whole world is unimportant when in dissolution).

OṀ ṢAḌAIŚVARYA–SAMUDRĀYAI NAMAḤ

...who has the auspicious marks of the six godly qualities (aiśvarya, affluence; vīrya, valour; yaśass, fame; śrī, auspciousness; jñānaṁ, knowledge; vairāgya, dispassion).

OṀ DŪRĪ–KṚTA–ṢAḌ–ŪRMAYE NAMAḤ

...who is devoid of the six modifications of life (birth, existence, growth, change or evolution, degeneration, destruction).

OṀ NITYA–PRABUDDHA–SAṀŚUDDHA–NIR–MUKTĀTMA–PRABHĀMUCE NAMAḤ

...who is emanating the light of the Self which is eternal, conscious, pure and free.

OṀ KĀRUṆYĀKULA–CITTĀYAI NAMAḤ

...who is full of mercy.

OṀ TYAKTA–YOGA–SUṢUPTAYE NAMAḤ

...who has given up the yogic sleep.

OṀ KERALA–KṢMĀVATĪRṆĀYAI NAMAḤ

...who has incarnated in the land of Kerala.

OṀ MĀNUṢA–STṚĪ–VAPURBHṚTE NAMAḤ

...who has a feminine human body.

OṀ DHARMIṢṬHA–SUGUṆĀNANDA–DAMAYANTĪ–SVAYAM–BHUVE NAMAḤ

...who has incarnated of Her own will as the daughter of the virtuous Sugunananda and Damayanti.

OṀ MĀTĀ–PITṚ–CIRĀCĪRṆA–PUNYA–PŪRA–PHALĀTMANE NAMAḤ

...who was born to Her parents as a result of their many virtuous lives.

OṀ NIŚŚABDA–JANANĪ–GARBHA–NIRGAMĀTBHUTA–KAṚMAṆE NAMAḤ

...who did the miraculous deed of keeping silence when She came out of Her mother's womb.

OṀ KĀLĪ–ŚRĪ–KṚṢṆA–SAṄKĀŚA–KOṀALA–ŚYĀMALA–TVIṢE NAMAḤ

...who has the beautiful dark complexion of Kali and Krishna.

OṀ CIRA–NAṢṬA–PUNAṚ–LABDHA–BHĀRGAVA–KṢETRA–SAMPADE NAMAḤ

...who is the wealth (treasure) of Kerala (land of Bhargava, an incarnation) which had been missing for a long time and has been regained.

OṀ MṚTA–PRĀYA–BHṚGU–KṢETṚA–PUNAR–UDDHITA–TEJASE NAMAḤ

...who is the life of the land of Kerala, which was almost dying and then rose back again.

OṀ SAUŚĪLYĀDI–GUṆĀKṚṢṬA–JAṄGAMA–STHĀVARĀLAYE NAMAḤ

...who by Her qualities like good behaviour etc. attract the whole creation (both moving and non-moving).

OṀ MANUṢYA–MṚGA–PAKṢYĀDI–SAṚVA–SAṀSEVITĀṄGHRAYE NAMAḤ

...whose feet are served by humans, animals, birds and all others.

OṀ NAISAṚGIKA–DAYĀ–TĪRTHA–SNĀNA–KLINNĀNTAR–ĀTMANE NAMAḤ

...whose mind is always bathing in the holy river of mercy.

OṀ DARIDRA–JANATĀ–HASTA–SAMARPITA–NIJĀNDHASE NAMAḤ

...who offered Her own food to the poor.

OṀ ANYA–VAKTRA–PRABHUKTTĀNNA–PŪRITA–SVĪYA–KUKṢAYE NAMAḤ

...whose need for food is fully satisfied when others have their meals.

OṀ SAṀPRĀPTA–SARVA–BHŪTĀTMA–SVĀTMA–SATTĀNUBHŪTAYE NAMAḤ

...who attained the experience of oneness with one and all.

OṀ AŚIKṢITA–SVAYAM–SVĀNTA–SPHURAT–KṚṢṆA–VIBHŪTAYE NAMAḤ

...who knew all about Krishna without being taught. (In whose mind dawned all the godly qualities of Krishna.)

OṀ ACCHINNA–MADHURŌDHĀRA–KṚṢṆA–LĪLĀNUSANDHAYE NAMAḤ

...who continuously contemplated on the various sports of Lord Krishna which brings sweet memories.

OṀ NANDĀTMAJA–MUKHĀLOKA–NITYOTKAṆṬHITA–CETASE NAMAḤ

...whose mind was ever craving to see the face of the Son (Krishna) of Nanda.

OṀ GOVINDA–VIPRAYOGĀDHI–DĀVA–DAGDĀNTAR–ĀTMANE NAMAḤ

...whose mind was burning in the fire of the agony of non-union with Govinda (Krishna).

OṀ VI–YOGA–ŚOKA–SAṀMŪRCCHĀ–MUHUR–PATITA–VARṢMAṆE NAMAḤ

...whose body was often falling down, unconscious due to the grief of non-union with Krishna.

OṀ SĀRAMEYĀDI–VIHITA–ŚUŚRŪṢĀ–LABDHA–BUDDHAYE NAMAḤ

...who regained consciousness by the proper nursing done by dogs and other animals.

OṀ PṚEMA–BHAKTI–BALĀKṚṢṬA–PRĀDUR–BHĀVITA–ŚĀRṄGIṆE NAMAḤ

...whose supreme love attracted Krishna by force, as it were, to manifest Himself before Her.

OṀ KṚṢṆĀ–LOKA–MAHĀHLĀDA–DHVASTA–ŚOKĀNTAR–ĀTMANE NAMAḤ

...whose mind was relieved of its agony by the immense joy of the vision of Krishna.

OṀ KĀÑCĪ–CANDRAKA–MANJĪRA–VAMŚĪ–ŚOBHI–SVA–BHŪ–DṚŚE NAMAḤ

...who had the vision of the form of Krishna shining with the golden ornaments hanging on His belt, anklets, peacock feather and flute.

OṀ SĀRVATRIKA–HṚṢĪKEŚA–SĀNNIDHYA–LAHARĪ–SPṚŚE NAMAḤ

...who felt the all-pervading presence of Rishikesha (another name for Krishna meaning one who has conquered all the senses).

OṀ SUSMERA–TAN–MUKHĀLOKA–VISMEROT-PHULLA–DṚṢṬAYE NAMAḤ...

whose eyes remained widely open with joy on beholding the smiling face (of Krishna).

OṀ TAT–KĀNTI–YAMUNĀ–SPARŚA–HṚṢṬA–ROṀĀṄGA–YAṢṬAYE NAMAḤ

...whose hair stood on end when She bathed in that emanating light (of Krishna) which was like the Yamuna river.

OṀ APRATĪKṢITA–SAṀPRĀPTA–DEVĪ–RŪPOPALABDHAYE NAMAḤ

...who had an unexpected vision of the form of the Divine Mother.

OṀ PĀṆĪ–PADMA–SVAPADVĪṆĀ–ŚOBHAMĀNĀMBIKĀDṚŚE NAMAḤ

...who had the vision of the Divine Mother's beautiful form holding the veena in Her lotus hand.

OṀ DEVĪ–SADYAS–TIRODHĀNA–TĀPA–VYADHITA–CETASE NAMAḤ

...who became extremely sorrowful on the Divine Mother's sudden disappearance.

OṀ DĪNA–RODANA–NIṚGHOṢA–DĪRṆA–DIKKARṆA–VARTHMANE NAMAḤ

...whose sorrowful wailing was tearing the ears of the four skies.

OṀ TYAKTĀNNA–PĀNA–NIDRĀDI–SARVA–DAIHIKA–DHARMAṆE NAMAḤ...

who gave up all thoughts of bodily activities like eating, drinking, sleeping, etc.

OṀ KURARĀDI–SAMĀNĪTA–BHAKṢYA–POṢITA–VARṢMAṆE NAMAḤ

...whose body was nourished by the food brought by birds and other animals.

OṀ VĪṆĀ–NIṢYANTI–SAṄGĪTA–LĀLITA–ŚṚUTI–NĀLAYE NAMAḤ

...whose ears became filled by the waves of divine melodies emanating from the veena (in the hands of the Divine Mother).

OṀ APĀRA–PARAMĀNANDA–LAHARĪ–MAGNA–CETASE NAMAḤ

...whose mind was merged in the intoxicating supreme bliss. (apara=limitless)

OṀ CAṆḌIKĀ–BHĪKARĀKĀRA–DARŚANĀLABDHA–ŚARMAṆE NAMAḤ

...who was unsatisfied by the vision of the terrible form of the Divine Mother (Chandika).

OṀ ŚĀNTA–RŪPĀMṚITAJHARĪ–PĀRAṆĀ–NIRVṚTĀTMANE NAMAḤ

...who was fully satisfied by drinking from the ambrosial river of the blissful aspect (of the Divine Mother).

OṀ ŚĀRADĀ–SMĀRAKĀŚEṢA–SVABHĀVA–GUṆA–SAṀPADE NAMAḤ

...whose nature and all qualities remind us of Sri Sarada Devi.

OṀ PRATIBIṀBITA–CĀNDREYA–ŚĀRADOBHAYA–MŪRTTAYE NAMAḤ

...in whom is reflected the forms of Sri Ramakrishna and Sarada Devi.

OṀ TANNĀḌAKĀBHINAYANA–NITYA–RAṄGĀYITĀTMANE NAMAḤ

...in whom we can see the play of these two re-enacted.

OṀ CĀNDREYĀ–ŚĀRADĀ–KELĪ–KALLOLITA–SUDHĀBDHAYE NAMAḤ

...who is the ocean of ambrosia in which the waves of the various plays of Sri Ramakrishna and Sarada Devi arise.

OṀ UTTEJITA–BHṚGU–KṢETRA–DAIVA–CAITANYA–RAMHASE NAMAḤ

...who has strengthened the divine potentialities of Kerala.

OṀ BHŪYAḤ–PRATYAVARUDDHĀRṢA–DIVYA–SAṀSKĀRA–RĀŚAYE NAMAḤ

...who has brought forth again the eternal values set by the rishis.

OṀ APRĀKṚTĀTBHUTĀNANDA–KALYĀṆA–GUṆA–SINDHAVE NAMAḤ

...who is an ocean of divine qualities which are wonderful and blissful.

OṀ AIŚVARYA–VĪRYA–KIṚTI–ŚRĪ–JÑĀNA–VAIRĀGYA–VEŚMAṆE NAMAḤ

...who is the embodiment of aisvarya (rulership), virya (valour), kirti (fame), sri (auspiciousness), jnana (knowledge) and vairagya (dispassion). (six characteristics of divine personification)

OṀ UPĀTTA–BĀLA–GOPĀLA–VEṢA–BHŪṢĀ–VIBHŪTAYE NAMAḤ

...who acquired the form and qualities of Bala Gopala (the child Krishna).

OṀ SMERA–SNIGDHA–KAḌĀKṢĀYAI NAMAḤ

...whose glances are most sweet and loving.

OṀ SVAIRĀDYUṢITA–VEDAYE NAMAḤ

...who in the form of Krishna plays freely (with the devotees).

OṀ PIÑCA–KUṆḌALA–MAÑJĪRA–VAṀŚIKĀ–KIṄKIṆI–BHṚTE NAMAḤ

...who wore all the ornaments, the peacock feather and the flute, like Krishna.

OṀ BHAKTA–LOKĀKHILĀ–BHĪṢṬA–PŪRAṆA–PṚĪṆANECCHAVE NAMAḤ...

who wishes to please Her devotees by fulfilling all their desires.

OṀ PĪṬHĀRŪḌHA–MAHĀDEVĪ–BHĀVA–BHĀSVARA–MŪRTTAYE NAMAḤ

...who in the mood of the Great Divine Mother, seated on the altar, shines with great effulgence.

OṀ BHŪṢANĀṀBARA–VEṢA–ŚRĪ–DĪPYA–MĀNĀṄGA–YAṢṬAYE NAMAḤ

...whose entire body shines, adorned by ornaments and unique dress like that of the Divine Mother.

OṀ SU–PṚASANNA–MUKHĀṀBHOJA–VARĀBHAYADA–PĀṆAYE NAMAḤ

...who has a bright, shining face as beautiful as a lotus flower and who holds Her hand in the posture of blessing.

OṀ KIRĪṬA–RAŚANĀKARṆA–PŪRA–SVARṆA–PAḌĪ–BHṚTE NAMAḤ

...who is wearing all the various gold ornaments and the crown like the Divine Mother.

OṀ JIHVA–LĪDHA–MAHĀ–ROGI–BĪBHATSA–VṚṆITA–TVACE NAMAḤ

...who with Her tongue touches the festering skin ulcers of many patients or persons with disease.

OṀ TVAG–ROGA–DHVAṀSA–NIṢṆĀTA–GAURĀNGĀPARA–MŪRTTAYE NAMAḤ

...who is like Sri Chaitanya in removing skin diseases.

OṀ STEYA–HIMSĀ–SURĀPĀNĀDYA-ŚEṢĀDHARMA–VIDVIṢE NAMAḤ

...who is strongly disapproving of bad qualities like stealing, injuring others, using intoxicants, etc.

OṀ TYĀGA–VAIRĀGYA–MAITRYĀDI–SARVA–SADVĀSANĀ–PUṢE NAMAḤ

...who encourages the development of good qualities like renunciation, dispassion, love, etc.

OṀ PĀDĀŚRITA–MANŌRŪDHA–DUSSAMSKĀRA–RAHOMUṢE NAMAḤ

...who steals away all the bad tendencies from the hearts of those who have taken refuge in Her.

OṀ PREMA–BHAKTI–SUDHĀSIKTA–SĀDHU–CITTA–GUHĀJJYUṢE NAMAḤ

...who resides in the cave of the hearts of those who have supreme devotion.

OṀ SUDHĀMANI–MAHĀ–NĀMNE NAMAḤ

...who has the great name Sudhamani.

OṀ SUBHĀṢITA–SUDHĀ–MUCE NAMAḤ

...whose speech is as sweet as ambrosia.

OṀ AMRITĀNANDA–MAYYĀKHYĀ–JANAKARṆA–PUTA–SPṚŚE NAMAḤ

...who in Her name Amritanandamayi is well known to the world.

OṀ DṚPTA–DATTA–VIRAKTĀYAI NAMAḤ

...who has aversion towards the offerings of vain and worldly people.

OṀ NAMRĀRPITA–BHUBHUKṢAVE NAMAḤ

...who accepts food offered with humility by devotees.

OṀ UṬSṚṢṬA–BHŌGI–SAṄGĀYAI NAMAḤ

...who avoids sensual people.

OṀ YOGI–SAṄGA–RIRAṀSAVE NAMAḤ

...who likes the company of yogis.

OṀ ABHINANDITA–DĀNĀDI–ŚUBHA–KARMĀ–BHIVṚDDHAYE NAMAḤ

...who encourages good actions like charity, etc.

OṀ ABHIVANDITA–NIŚŚEṢA–STHIRA–JANGAMA–SṚṢṬAYE NAMAḤ

...who is worshipped by the sentient and insentient beings of the world.

OṀ PRŌTSĀHITA–BRAHMA–VIDYĀ–SAMPRADĀYA–PRAVṚTTAYE NAMAḤ

...who encourages the learning that will lead to truth.

OṀ PUNARĀSĀDITA–ŚREṢṬHA–TAPŌVIPINA–VṚTTAYE NAMAḤ

...who brought back the great way of living of the sages of the forests.

OṀ BHŪYO–GURUKULĀ–VĀSA–ŚIKṢAṆOTSUKA–MEDHASE NAMAḤ

...who is very much interested in re-establishing the 'gurukula' way of education.

OṀ ANEKA–NAIṢṬIKA–BRAHMACĀRI–NIRMĀTṚ–VEDHASE NAMAḤ

...who is a mother to many, many life-long brahmacharins.

OṀ ŚIṢYA–SAMKRĀMITA–SVĪYA–PROJVALAT–BRAHMA–VARCASE NAMAḤ

...who has given the divine brilliance to Her disciples.

OṀ ANTEVĀSI–JANĀŚEṢA–CEṢṬĀ–PĀTITA–DṚṢṬAYE NAMAḤ

...who sees all the actions of the disciples.

OṀ MOHĀNDHA–KĀRA–SAÑCĀRI–LOKĀNUGRĀHI–ROCIṢE NAMAḤ

...who delights in blessing the worlds like a lamp which removes darkness.

OṀ TAMAḤ–KLIṢṬA–MANŌ–VṚṢṬA–SVAPRAKĀŚA–ŚUBHĀŚIṢE NAMAḤ

...who is the light for the ignorant.

OṀ BHAKTA–ŚUDDHĀNṬA–RAṄGASTHA–BHADRA–DĪPA–ŚIKHĀ–TVIṢE NAMAḤ

...who is the bright flame of the lamp kindled in the pure hearts of devotees.

OṀ SAPRĪTHI–BHUKTA -BHAKTAUGHANYARPITA–SNEHA–SARPIṢE NAMAḤ

...who enjoys taking the ghee (butter) of the devotees' love.

OṀ ŚIṢYA–VARYA–SABHĀ–MADHYA–DHYĀNA–YOGA–VIDHITSAVE NAMAḤ

...who likes to sit with the disciples in meditation.

OṀ ŚAŚVALLOKA–HITĀCĀRA–MAGNA–DEHENDRIYĀSAVE NAMAḤ

...who is always concerned with the good of the world.

OṀ NIJA–PUṆYA–PRADĀNĀNYA–PĀPĀDĀNA–CIKĪRṢAVE NAMAḤ

...who is happy in exchanging Her own merits with the demerits of others.

OṀ PARA–SVARYĀPANA–SVĪYA–NARAKA–PRĀPTI–LIPSAVE NAMAḤ

...who is happy in exchanging heaven with hell for the relief of others.

OṀ RATHOTSAVA–CALAT–KANYĀ–KUMĀRĪ–MARTYA–MŪRTTAYE NAMAḤ

...who is Kanya Kumari (goddess of Cape Comarin) in human form.

OṀ VIMŌHĀRṆAVA–NIRMAGNA-BHṚGU–KṢETROJJIHĪRṢAVE NAMAḤ

...who is anxious to bring up the land of Kerala which is immersed in the ocean of ignorance.

OṀ PUNASSANTĀNITA–DVAIPĀYANA–SATKULA–TANTAVE NAMAḤ

...who has given a high place to this community of fishermen by taking birth in their line which is supposed to be the line of the great sage Vyasa.

OṀ VEDA–ŚĀSTRA–PURĀṆETIHĀSA–ŚĀŚVATA–BANDHAVE NAMAḤ

...who promotes the vedic knowledge and all other spiritual texts.

OṀ BṚGHU–KṢETRA–SAMUNMĪLAT–PARA–DAIVATA–TEJASE NAMAḤ

...who is the divine consciousness of the the awakening of the land of Kerala.

OṀ DEVYAI NAMAḤ

...who is the Great Divine Mother.

OṀ PREMĀMRITĀNANDAMAYYAI–NITYAM–NAMO NAMAḤ

...who is full of divine love and bliss.

108 Names of Devi, the Divine Mother

-MEDITATION-

SINDŪR ĀRUNA VIGRAHĀM TRINAYANĀM
MĀNIKYA MAULI SPHURAT
TĀRĀ NĀYAKA ŚEKHARĀM
SMITA MUKHĪM ĀPĪNA VAKṢORUHĀM
PĀNIBHYĀM ALIPŪRṆA RATNA CHAṢAKAM
RAKTŌTPALAM BIBHRATĪM
SAUMYĀM RATNA GHATASTHA RAKTA
CARANĀM DHYĀYET PARĀM AMBIKĀM

DHYĀYET PADMĀSANASTHĀM
VIKASITA VADANĀM PADMA PATRĀYA TĀKSHĪM
HEMĀBHĀM PĪTA VASTRĀM KARAKALI TALASAT
HEMAPADMĀM VARĀNGĪṀ

SARVĀLAṄKĀRA YUKTĀM SATATAM ABHAYATĀM
BHAKTANAMRĀM BHAVĀNĪṀ
ŚRĪ VIDYĀM ṢĀNTA MŪRTĪṀ SAKALA SURANUTĀM
SARVA SAMPAT PRADĀTRĪṀ

SAKUMKUMA VILEPANĀ
MALLIKA CHUMBI KASTŪRIKĀM
SAMANDA HASITEKṢANĀM
SAŚARA CHĀPA PĀŚĀMKUŚĀM
ASEṢA JANA MŌHINĪM
ARUNA MĀLYA BHŪṢŌJVALĀM
JAPĀ KUSUMA BHĀSURĀM
JAPAVIDHAU SMARETAMBIKĀM

ARUNĀM KARUNĀM
TARAṄGI TĀKSHĪM
DHRITA PĀŚĀM
KUŚA PUṢPA BĀNA CHĀPĀM
ANIMĀDIBHI RĀVRATĀM MAYŪKHAI
RAHAMITYEVA VIBHĀVAYET MAHESĪM

She has three eyes; Her hue is like that of red sindura; the diadem of precious stones She wears has a crescent on it shining wonderfully.

That She is easily accessible is indicated by Her benign smile; Her children have an inexhaustible store of the milk of life in Her full breast; the vessel of honey in one hand and the red lotus in the other symbolize joy and wisdom of which She alone is the source; and Her feet placed on the precious pot full of valuable gems indicate that these are not difficult for those who surrender to Her feet and take refuge in Her.

I meditate upon Sri Bhavani Who is seated in the lotus of expansive countenance, Whose eyes are like lotus petals, Who is golden-hued, Who wears a yellow raiment, Who has in Her hand lotus flowers of gold, Who always dispels fear, Whose devotees bow before Her, Who is the embodiment of peace, Who is Sri Vidya Herself Who is praised by the Gods, and Who gives every wealth that is sought . .

I meditate on the Mother Whose eyes are smiling a little, Who has in Her hands the arrow, the bow, the noose and goad, Who bewitches everybody, Who is glittering with red garlands and ornaments, Who is painted with vermillion, Whose forehead is kissed with the mark of musk and Who is red and tender like the japa flower . . .

I meditate on the great Empress who is light red in color, Whose eyes are full of compassion, Who has in Her hands the noose, the goad, the bow and the flowery arrow and Who is surrounded on all sides by powers, such as 'anima,' like rays, as if She is the Self within me . . .

OṀ ŚRĪ LALITĀMBIKĀYAI NAMAḤ
Salutations to the Supreme Goddess Śri Lalitambika

OṀ ŚRĪ MĀTRE NAMAḤ
Salutations to the Sacred Mother

OṀ ŚRĪ MAHĀ RĀGNYAI NAMAḤ
Salutations to the Great Empress

OṀ BHAVĀNYAI NAMAḤ
Salutations to the Consort of Śiva

OṀ BHĀVANĀ GAMYĀYAI NAMAḤ
Salutations to the Mother Who is reached through constant reflection on Truth

OṀ BHADRA PRIYĀYAI NAMAḤ
Salutations to the Mother Who loves to be benevolent

OṀ BHADRA MÛRTYAI NAMAḤ
Salutations to the Mother Who is the embodiment of benevolence

OṀ BHAKTI PRIYĀYAI NAMAḤ
Salutations to the Mother Who is pleased by Her devotees' loving worship

OṀ BHAKTI GAMYĀYAI NAMAḤ
Salutations to the Mother Who is reached by yearning service and meditation

OṀ BHAKTI VASYĀYAI NAMAḤ
Salutations to the Mother Who is made one's own by loving acts of devotion

OṀ BHAYĀ PAHĀYAI NAMAḤ
Salutations to the Mother Who dispels all fear

OṀ ŚĀMBHAVYAI NAMAḤ
Salutations to the Mother Who worships Śambhu

OṀ ŚĀRADĀRĀDHYĀYAI NAMAḤ
Salutations to the Mother Who is worshipped as the Goddess of learning in the autumn

OṀ ŚARVĀNYAI NAMAḤ
Salutations to the Mother Who is the Consort of Sarva

OṀ ŚARMADĀYINYAI NAMAḤ
Salutations to the Mother Who is always the giver of happiness

OṀ ŚAṄKARYAI NAMAḤ
Salutations to the Mother Who is inseparable from Parama Śiva

OṀ ŚRĪKARYAI NAMAḤ
Salutations to the Mother Who is Vishnu's Consort, Laksmi

OṀ ŚĀTŌDARYAI NAMAḤ
Salutations to the Mother Who has a slender waist

OṀ ŚĀNTIMATYAI NAMAḤ
Salutations to the Mother Who is ever at peace with Her devotees

OṀ NIRĀDHĀRĀYAI NAMAḤ
Salutations to the Mother Who has no other support

OṀ NIRANJANĀYAI NAMAḤ
Salutations to the Mother Who is unstained

OṀ NIRLEPĀYAI NAMAḤ
Salutations to the Mother Who is untouched

OṀ NIRMALĀYAI NAMAḤ
Salutations to the Mother Who is ever pure

OṀ NITYĀYAI NAMAḤ
Salutations to the Mother Who is eternal

OṀ NIRĀKĀRĀYAI NAMAḤ
Salutations to the Mother Who is without form

OṀ NIRĀKULĀYAI NAMAḤ
Salutations to the Mother Who is never perturbed

OṀ NIRGUNĀYAI NAMAḤ
Salutations to the Mother Who is attributeless

OṀ NIṢKALĀYAI NAMAḤ
Salutations to the Mother Who is indivisible

OṀ ŚĀNTĀYAI NAMAḤ
Salutations to the Mother Who is perfectly serene

OṀ NIṢKĀMĀYAI NAMAḤ
Salutations to the Mother Who is free from all desires

OṀ NITYAMUKTĀYAI NAMAḤ
Salutations to the Mother Who is eternally free

OṀ NIRVIKĀRĀYAI NAMAḤ
Salutations to the Mother Who is the unchanging basis for all change

OṀ NIṢPRAPANCĀYAI NAMAḤ
Salutations to the Mother Who is beyond all phenomena of the world

OṀ NIRĀŚRAYĀYAI NAMAḤ
Salutations to the Mother Who depends on none

OṀ NITYA ŚUDDHĀYAI NAMAḤ
Salutations to the Mother Who is taintless

OṀ NITYA BUDDHĀYAI NAMAḤ
Salutations to the Mother Who is the perpetual abode of knowledge

OṀ NIRAVADYĀYAI NAMAḤ
Salutations to the Mother Who is entirely free from flaw

OṀ NIRANTARĀYAI NAMAḤ
Salutations to the Mother Who is without end

OṀ NIṢKĀRANĀYAI NAMAḤ
Salutations to the Mother Who is without beginning

OṀ NIṢKALANKĀYAI NAMAḤ
Salutations to the Mother Who has no lapse whatsoever

OṀ NIRUPĀDHĀYE NAMAḤ
Salutations to the Mother Who is limitless

OṀ NIRĪŚVARĀYAI NAMAḤ
Salutations to the Mother Who is supreme

OṀ NĪRĀGĀYAI NAMAḤ
Salutations to the Mother Who has no passions

OṀ RĀGA MATHANYAI NAMAḤ
Salutations to the Mother Who destroys all attachments

OṀ NIRMADĀYAI NAMAḤ
Salutations to the Mother Who has no pride

OṀ MADANĀŚINYAI NAMAḤ
Salutations to the Mother Who wipes out arrogance

OṀ NIŚCINTĀYAI NAMAḤ
Salutations to the Mother Who is free from all anxiety

OṀ NIRAHANKĀRĀYAI NAMAḤ
Salutations to the Mother Who is completely free from ego

OṀ NIRMŌHĀYAI NAMAḤ
Salutations to the Mother Who is completely free of delusion

OṀ MŌHA NĀŚINYAI NAMAḤ
Salutations to the Mother Who cures the delusions of Her devotees

OṀ NIRMAMĀYAI NAMAḤ
Salutations to the Mother Who has no "I"-ness or "my"-ness

OṀ MAMATĀ HANTRYAI NAMAḤ

Salutations to the Mother Who destroys conceit and selfishness in Her devotees

OṀ NIṢPĀPĀYAI NAMAḤ

Salutations to the Mother Who is the negation of sin

OṀ PĀPA NĀŚINYAI NAMAḤ

Salutations to the Mother Who completely destroys sin by the mere repetition of Her name

OṀ NIṢKRŌDHĀYAI NAMAḤ

Salutations to the Mother Who has no enemy or anger

OṀ KRŌDHA ŚAMANYAI NAMAḤ

Salutations to the Mother Who extinguishes anger rising in the minds of Her devotees

OṀ NIRLŌBHĀYAI NAMAḤ

Salutations to the Mother Who is completely free from greed

OṀ LŌBHA NĀŚINYAI NAMAḤ

Salutations to the Mother Who removes greed from the minds of Her devotees

OṀ NIHSAMŚAYĀYAI NAMAḤ

Salutations to the Mother Who is free from doubt

OṀ NIRBHAVĀYAI NAMAḤ

Salutations to the Mother Who has no origin

OṀ BHAVA NĀŚINYAI NAMAḤ

Salutations to the Mother Who puts an end to the round of birth and death

OṀ NIRVIKALPĀYAI NAMAḤ

Salutations to the Mother Who is the eternal pure Intelligence

OṀ NIRĀBĀDHĀYAI NAMAḤ

Salutations to the Mother Who remains ever untroubled

OṀ NIRBHEDĀYAI NAMAḤ

Salutations to the Mother in Whom all are absolutely One

OṀ BHEDA NĀŚINYAI NAMAḤ

Salutations to the Mother Who destroys the distinctions made by body-mind-intellect

OṀ NIRNĀŚĀYAI NAMAḤ

Salutations to the Mother Who is immortal

OṀ MṚTYU MATHANYAI NAMAḤ

Salutations to the Mother Who uproots the cause of death in Her devotees

OṀ NIṢKRIYĀYAI NAMAḤ

Salutations to the Mother Who is beyond all action

OṀ NIṢPARIGRAHĀYAI NAMAḤ

Salutations to the Mother Who takes nothing

OṀ NISTULĀYAI NAMAḤ

Salutations to the Mother Who is unequalled.

OṀ NĪLA CIKURĀYAI NAMAḤ

Salutations to the Mother Who has locks of shining black hair

OṀ NIRAPĀYĀYAI NAMAḤ

Salutations to the Mother Who never departs

OṀ NIRATYAYĀYAI NAMAḤ

Salutations to the Mother Who is beyond all danger

OṀ DURLABHĀYAI NAMAḤ

Salutations to the Mother Who is attained through long-sustained and necessary efforts

OṀ DURGAMĀYAI NAMAḤ

Salutations to the Mother Who is not reached without painstaking continued exertion

OṀ DURGĀYAI NAMAḤ

Salutations to the Mother Who is the Goddess Durga

OṀ DUKHA HANTRYAI NAMAḤ

Salutations to the Mother Who destroys sorrow

OṀ SUKHA PRADĀYAI NAMAḤ

Salutations to the Mother Who confers the bliss of liberation

OṀ SARVAGÑĀYAI NAMAḤ

Salutations to the Mother Who is Omniscient

OṀ SĀNDRA KARUNĀYAI NAMAḤ

Salutations to the Mother Who is intensely compassionate

OṀ SARVA ŚAKTI MAYYAI NAMAḤ

Salutations to the Mother Who is the source of all power

OṀ SARVA MAṄGALĀYAI NAMAḤ
Salutations to the Mother Who possesses all that is auspicious

OṀ SAD GATI PRADĀYAI NAMAḤ
Salutations to the Mother Who takes the seeker to the Supreme Goal

OṀ SARVEŚVARYAI NAMAḤ
Salutations to the Mother Who is the Queen of the Universe

OṀ SARVAMAYYAI NAMAḤ
Salutations to the Mother Who is immanent in all

OṀ MAHEŚVARYAI NAMAḤ
Salutations to the Mother Who transcends nature and is the source of all

OṀ MAHĀ KĀLYAI NAMAḤ
Salutations to the Mother Who is the Great Goddess Kali Who destroys even Death

OṀ MAHĀ DEVYAI NAMAḤ
Salutations to the Mother Who is the Greatest of Goddesses

OṀ MAHĀ LAKṢMYAI NAMAḤ
Salutations to the Mother Who is the Great Goddess Laksmi Who is the source of life's bounty

OṀ MAHĀ RŪPĀYAI NAMAḤ
Salutations to the Mother Who is the Supreme Form

OṀ MAHĀ PŪJYĀYAI NAMAḤ
Salutations to the Mother Who is worthy of supreme worship

OṀ MAHĀ MAYĀYAI NAMAḤ
Salutations to the Mother Who is the Supreme Creatrix of illusion

OṀ MAHĀ SATTVĀYAI NAMAḤ
Salutations to the Mother Who is the Supreme Existence

OṀ MAHĀ ŚAKTYAI NAMAḤ
Salutations to the Mother Who is the Supreme Energy

OM MAHĀ RATYAI NAMAḤ
Salutations to the Mother Who is boundless bliss

OṀ MAHĀ BHŌGĀYAI NAMAḤ
Salutations to the Mother Who is the supreme enjoyment and luxury

OṀ MAHAIŚVARYĀYAI NAMAḤ

Salutations to the Mother Who has supreme dominion

OṀ MAHĀ VIRYĀYAI NAMAḤ

Salutations to the Mother of supreme prowess and strength

OṀ MAHĀ BALĀYAI NAMAḤ

Salutations to the Mother Who is of great strength

OṀ MAHĀ BUDDHYAI NAMAḤ

Salutations to the Mother Who is supreme intelligence

OṀ MAHĀ SIDDHYAI NAMAḤ

Salutations to the Mother Whose attainments are supreme

OṀ MAHĀ TANTRĀYAI NAMAḤ

Salutations to the Mother Who is the subject of the supreme mystical texts

OṀ MAHĀ MANTRĀYAI NAMAḤ

Salutations to the Mother Who is the supreme mantra

OṀ MAHĀ YANTRĀYAI NAMAHĀ

Salutations to the Mother Who is worshipped in the supreme mystic symbols

OṀ MAHĀSANĀYAI NAMAḤ

Salutations to the Mother Whose seat is worthy of the highest worship

OṀ PARAM JYŌTYAI NAMAḤ

Salutations to the Mother Who is the Supreme Radiance

OṀ PARAM DHĀMNE NAMAḤ

Salutations to the Mother Who is the Supreme Abode

OṀ PARAMĀNAVE NAMAḤ

Salutations to the Mother Who is subtler than the subtlest

OṀ PARĀT PARĀYAI NAMAḤ

Salutations to the Mother Who is greater than the greatest

OṀ PARĀ ŚAKTYAI NAMAḤ

Salutations to the Mother Who is the supreme absolute energy

OṀ ŚRĪ ŚIVĀYAI NAMAḤ

Salutations to the Mother Who is the most worshipful Śiva

OṀ ŚIVA ŚAKTYAIKYA RŪPINYAI NAMAḤ

Salutations to the Mother Who is not different from the unity of Śiva and Śakti

OṀ VIṢṆU ŚAKTYAIKYA RŪPINYAI NAMAḤ

Salutations to the Mother Who is not different from the union of Vishnu and Śakti

OṀ BRAHMA ŚAKTYAIKYA RŪPINYAI NAMAḤ

Salutations to the Mother Who is not different from the unity of Brahma and Śakti

OṀ ŚRĪ LALITĀMBIKĀYAI NAMAḤ

Salutations to the Supreme Goddess Sri Lalitambika

OṀ ŚRĪ MĀTĀ AMRITĀNANDAMĀYE NAMAḤ

Salutations to the Mother Amritanandamayi

OṀ ŚRĪ MAHĀ TRIPURA SUNDARYAI NAMAḤ

Salutations to the Supreme Venerable Mother Tripurasundari

108 Names of Sri Krishna

OṀ ŚRĪ KṚṢṆĀYA NAMAḤ

Salutations to Sri Krishna

OṀ KAMALĀ NĀTHĀYA NAMAḤ

...to Kamala's (Sri Lakshmi's) spouse (Lord)

OṀ VĀSUDEVĀYA NAMAḤ

...to Vasudeva (Vasudeva's son)

OṀ SANĀTANĀYA NAMAḤ

...to the Eternal One

OṀ VASUDEVAYA NAMAḤ

...to the Son of Vasudeva

OṀ PUṆYĀYA NAMAḤ

...to the meritorious one

OṀ LĪLĀ-MĀNUṢA-VIGRAHĀYA NAMAḤ

...to Him who has assumed a human form to carry out His leelas

OṀ ŚRĪVATSA KAUSTHUBHA-DHARĀYA NAMAḤ

...to the Lord who wears the Sree Vatsa (a golden streak representing Sri Lakshmi) and the Kaustubha gem

OṀ YAŚODĀ-VATSALĀYA NAMAḤ
...to Yasoda's darling Child

OṀ HARAYE NAMAḤ
...to Sri Hari (Vishnu)

OṀ CATURBHUJĀTTA-CAKRĀSI-GADĀ-ŚAṄKĀDHYĀYUD HĀYA NAMAḤ
...to the Four-armed One who carries the weapons of discus, conch and club

OṀ DEVAKĪ NANDANĀYA NAMAḤ
...to Devaki's son

OṀ ŚRĪSĀYA NAMAḤ
...to the abode of Sri (Lakshmi)

OṀ NANDAGOPA PRIYĀTMAJĀYA NAMAḤ
...to Nanda Gopa's darling child

OṀ YAMUNĀVEGA SAṀHĀRIṆE NAMAḤ
...to the Lord who destroyed the speed of the river Yamuna

OṀ BALABHADRA PRIYĀNUJĀYA NAMAḤ
...to Balabhadra's (Balarama's) dear younger brother

OṀ PŪTANĀ JĪVITA HARĀYA NAMAḤ
...to the Destroyer of the demoness Putana

OṀ ŚAKATĀSURA BHAÑJANĀYA NAMAḤ
...to the Lord who destroyed the demon Sakatasura

OṀ NANDAVRAJA JANĀ NANDINE NAMAḤ
...to the Lord who brought great happiness to Nanda andthe people of Vraja

OṀ SACCIDĀNANDA VIGRAHĀYA NAMAḤ
...to the Lord who is the embodiment of Existence, Awareness and Bliss

OṀ NAVANĪTA VILIPTĀṄGĀYA NAMAḤ
...to the Lord whose body is smeared with butter

OṀ NAVANĪTA NATĀYA NAMAḤ
...to the One who danced to get butter

OṀ ĀNAGHĀYA NAMAḤ
...to the sinless One

OṀ NAVANĪTA NAVĀHĀRĀYA NAMAḤ

...to the Lord who invented a new form of food--butter (because he consumed large quantities of it)

OṀ MUCUKUNDA PRASĀDAKĀYA NAMAḤ

...to the Lord who blessed (gave salvation) King Muchukunda

OṀ ŚODAŚA STHRĪ SAHASREŚĀYA NAMAḤ

... to the Lord of sixteen thousand women

OṀ TRIBHAṄGĪ LALITĀKRITAYE NAMAḤ

...to the Lord who is bent at three places (a pose of Krishna's)

OṀ ŚUKAVĀG AMṚTĀBHDHĪNDAVE NAMAḤ

...to the ocean of nectar in the form of Sukadeva's words (refers to Sukadeva's narration of Srimad Bhagavata to King Parikshit)

OṀ GOVINDĀYA NAMAḤ

...to Lord of the cows

OṀ YOGĪNĀM PATAYE NAMAḤ

...to the Lord of the yogis

OṀ VATSA VATĀCARĀYA NAMAḤ

...to the Lord who roamed around (Vrindavana) in the company of calves and gopa boys

OṀ ANANTĀYA NAMAḤ

...to the Infinite One

OṀ DHENUKĀSURA MARDANĀYA NAMAḤ

...to the Lord who killed the demon

OṀ TṚṆĪKṚTA TṚṆĀVARTĀYA NAMAḤ

...to the Lord who destroyed the whirlwind demon Trinavarta

OṀ YAMALĀRJUNA BHAÑJANĀYA NAMAḤ

...to the Lord who broke the two Yamalarjuna trees which were really the two celestial beings who had been cursed

OṀ UTTĀLA TĀLABHETTRE NAMAḤ

...to the Lord who broke the huge trees

OṀ TAMĀLA ŚYĀMALĀ KṚTAYE NAMAḤ

...to the Lord who is as beautiful as the dark Tamala tree

OṀ GOPA GOPĪŚVARĀYA NAMAḤ

...to the Lord of Gopas and Gopis

OṀ YOGINE NAMAḤ

...to the (greatest) Yogi

OṀ KOTI SŪRYA SAMAPRABHĀYA NAMAḤ

...to the Lord who is as lustrous as a million Suns

OṀ ILĀPATAYE NAMAḤ

...to the Lord of the Earth

OṀ PARASMAI JYOTIṢE NAMAḤ

...to the One who is the Supreme Light

OṀ YĀDAVENDRĀYA NAMAḤ

...to the Lord of the Yadavas

OṀ YADUDVAHĀYA NAMAḤ

...to the Leader of the Yadus

OṀ VANAMĀLINE NAMAḤ

...to the Lord who wears a sylvan garland

OṀ PĪTA VĀSASE NAMAḤ

...to the Lord who wears Yellow (golden) robes

OṀ PĀRIJĀTĀPA HĀRAKĀYA NAMAḤ

...to the Lord who removed the Parijatha flower (from Indra's garden)

OṀ GOVARDHANĀCALO DHARTRE NAMAḤ

...to the Lord who lifted the Govardhana Mountain

OṀ GOPĀLĀYA NAMAḤ

...to the Protector of the cows

OṀ SARVA PĀLAKĀYA NAMAḤ

...to the protector of all (created beings)

OṀ AJĀYA NAMAḤ

...to the Lord who is ever victorious

OṀ NIRAÑJANĀYA NAMAḤ

...to the Lord who is untainted

OṀ KĀMA JANAKĀYA NAMAḤ

...to the Lord who generates desires in the worldly-minded

OṀ KAÑCA LOCANĀYA NAMAḤ

...to the Lord who has beautiful eyes

OṀ MADHUGHNE NAMAḤ

...to the Lord who killed the demon Madhu

OṀ MATHURĀ NĀTHĀYA NAMAḤ
...to the Lord of Mathura

OṀ DVĀRAKĀ NĀYAKĀYA NAMAḤ
...to the Lord of Dwaraka

OṀ BALINE NAMAḤ
...to the all powerful Lord

OṀ BRINDĀVANĀNTA SAÑCĀRIṆE NAMAḤ
...to the Lord who roamed around Vrindavana

OṀ TULASIDĀMA BHŪṢAṆĀYA NAMAḤ
...to the Lord who adorns Himself with tulasi leaves (a garland)

OṀ SYAMANTAKA MAṆER HARTRE NAMAḤ
...to the Lord who stole the Syamantaka gem

OṀ NARA NĀRĀYAṆĀTMAKĀYA NAMAḤ
...to the Lord who has the twin forms of Nara and Narayana

OṀ KUBJĀ KṚṢṬĀMBARADHARĀYA NAMAḤ
...to the Lord who wore the unguent offered by the hunchbacked lady

OṀ MĀYINE NAMAḤ
...to the Lord who is Maya (delusion)

OṀ PARAMAPŪRUṢĀYA NAMAḤ
...to the Supreme Person

OṀ MUṢṬIKĀSURA CĀṆŪRA MALLAYUDHA-VIŚĀRADĀYA NAMAḤ
...to the expert wrestler who wrestled with the two demons, Mushtika and Chanura

OṀ SAMSĀRA VAIRIṆE NAMAḤ
...to the enemy of Samsara (the cycle of births and deaths)

OṀ KAMSĀRAYE NAMAḤ
...to the enemy of Kamsa

OṀ MURĀRAYE NAMAḤ
...to the enemy of the demon Mura

OṀ NARAKĀNTAKĀYA NAMAḤ
...to the destroyer of the demon Naraka

OṀ ANĀDI BRAHMACĀRIṆE NAMAḤ
...to the beginningless Absolute

OṀ KṚṢṆĀ VYASANA KARŚAKĀYA NAMAḤ
...to the One who removed Draupadi's distress

OṀ ŚIŚUPĀLA ŚIRASCETTRE NAMAḤ
...to the Lord who cut off Sisupala's head

OṀ DURYODHANA KULĀNTAKĀYA NAMAḤ
...to the destroyer of the dynasty of Duryodhana

OṀ VIDURĀKRŪRA VARADĀYA NAMAḤ
...to the Lord who gave boons to Vidura and Akrura

OṀ VIŚVARŪPA PRADĀRŚAKĀYA NAMAḤ
...to the Lord who exhibited His Viswarupa (the Universal Form)

OṀ SATYAVĀCE NAMAḤ
...to the Lord who utters only truth

OṀ SATYA SAṄKALPĀYA NAMAḤ
...to the Lord of true resolve

OṀ SATYABHĀMA RATĀYA NAMAḤ
...to the Lover of Satyabhama

OṀ JAYINE NAMAḤ
...to the Lord who is ever victorious

OṀ SUBHADRA PŪRVAJĀYA NAMAḤ
...to the elder brother of Subhadra

OṀ VIṢṆAVE NAMAḤ
...to Lord Vishnu

OṀ BHĪṢMA MUKTI PRADĀYAKĀYA NAMAḤ
...to the Lord who bestowed salvation on Bhishma

OṀ JAGADGURAVE NAMAḤ
...to the Lord who is Guru to the whole world

OṀ JAGANNĀTHĀYA NAMAḤ
...to the Lord of the whole world

OṀ VEṆUNĀDA VIŚĀRADĀYA NAMAḤ
...to the Lord who is an expert in flute music

OṀ VṚṢABHĀSURA VIDHVAṀSINE NAMAḤ
...to the Lord who destroyed the demon Vrishaba

OṀ BĀṆĀSURA KARĀNTAKĀYA NAMAḤ

...to the Lord who chopped off the demon Bana's hands

OṀ YUDHIṢṬHIRA PRATIṢṬHĀTRE NAMAḤ

...to the Lord who established Yudhishtira (as the King)

OṀ BĀRHI BĀRHĀVATAṀSAKĀYA NAMAḤ

...to the One who is adorned with effulgent peacock feathers

OṀ PARTHASĀRATHĀYE NAMAḤ

...to the charioteer of Arjuna

OṀ AVYAKTĀYA NAMAḤ

...to the Lord who is difficult to comprehend

OṀ GĪTĀMṚTA MAHODADHAYE NAMAḤ

...to the Ocean containing the nectar of the Bhagavad Gita

OṀ KĀLĪYAPHAṆI MĀṆIKYA RAÑJITA ŚRĪ PADĀMBHUJĀYA NAMAḤ

...to the Lord whose lotus feet are adorned with the gems from the hoods of the serpent Kaliya

OṀ DĀMODARĀYA NAMAḤ

...to the One who was tied with a grinding stone around His waist

OṀ YAJÑABHOKTRE NAMAḤ

...to the Lord who consumes sacrificial offerings

OṀ DĀNAVENDRA VINĀŚAKĀYA NAMAḤ

...to the Destroyer of the Lord of Asuras

OṀ NĀRĀYAṆĀYA NAMAḤ

...to Lord Narayana

OṀ PARABRAHMAṆE NAMAḤ

...to the Supreme Brahman

OṀ PANNAGĀŚANA VĀHANĀYA NAMAḤ

...to the Lord who has a serpent (Adisesha) as His seat

OṀ JALAKRĪDĀSAMĀŚAKTA GOPI VASTRĀPAHĀRAKĀYA NAMAḤ

...to the Lord who (playfully) hid the clothes (left on the shore) of the gopis who were engrossed in playing in the waters of the river Yamuna

OṀ PUṆYA-ŚLOKĀYA NAMAḤ

...to the Lord whose praises bestow merit

OṀ TIRTHAPĀDĀYA NAMAḤ
...to the One whose Feet are holy

OṀ VEDAVEDYĀYA NAMAḤ
...to the source of the Vedas

OṀ DAYĀNIDHAYE NAMAḤ
...to the Treasure of Compassion

OṀ SARVA BHŪTĀTMAKĀYA NAMAḤ
...to the Soul of the elements

OṀ SARVAGRAHA RŪPIṆE NAMAḤ
...to the All-formed One

OṀ PARĀTPARĀYA NAMAḤ
...to the One who is highest than the highest

108 Names of Siva

OṀ ŚIVĀYA NAMAḤ
Hail to the Auspicious One

OṀ MAHEŚVARĀYA NAMAḤ
Praise the Supreme God Śiva

OṀ ŚAMBHAVE NAMAḤ
To the God who exists for our happiness alone, prostrations!

OṀ PINĀKINE NAMAḤ
Hail to Śiva, who guards the path of dharma

OṀ ŚAŚIŚEKHARĀYA NAMAḤ
Praise the God who wears the crescent moon in His hair

OṀ VĀMADEVĀYA NAMAḤ
Hail to the God who is pleasing and auspicious in every way

OṀ VIRUPĀKṢĀYA NAMAḤ
Prostrations to the God of spotless form!

OṀ KAPARDINE NAMAḤ
Praise the Lord of thickly matted hair.

OṀ NĪLALOHITĀYA NAMAḤ
To God, splendid as the red sun at daybreak, prostrations!

OṀ ŚANKARĀYA NAMAḤ

Hail to the source of all prosperity.

OṀ ŚŪLAPĀṆAYE NAMAḤ

Praise the God who carries a spear.

OṀ KHATVĀṄGINE NAMAḤ

To the God who carries a knurled club, prostrations!

OṀ VIṢṆUVALLABHĀYA NAMAḤ

Hail to Śiva, who is dear to Lord Vishnu.

OṀ ŚIPIVIṢṬĀYA NAMAḤ

Praise the Lord whose form emits great rays of light.

OṀ AMBIKĀNĀTHĀYA NAMAḤ

To Ambika's Lord, prostrations!

OṀ ŚRĪKAṆṬĀYA NAMAḤ

Hail to God, whose throat is shining blue.

OṀ BHAKTAVATSALĀYA NAMAḤ

To the Lord who loves His devotees like new born calves.

OṀ BHAVĀYA NAMAḤ

The God who is existence itself, prostrations!

OṀ SARVĀYA NAMAḤ

Hail to Śiva, who is the All.

OṀ TRILOKEŚĀYA NAMAḤ

Praise God Śiva, who is the Lord of all the three worlds.

OṀ ŚITIKAṆṬHĀYA NAMAḤ

To the Primal Soul, whose throat is deep blue, prostrations!

OṀ ŚIVĀPRIYĀYA NAMAN

Hail to God, who is dear toŚakti.

OṀ UGRĀYA NAMAḤ

Praise Śiva, whose presence is awesome and overwhelming.

OṀ KAPĀLINE NAMAḤ

To the God whose begging bowl is a human skull, prostrations!

OṀ KĀMĀRAYE NAMAḤ

Hail to Śiva, who conquers all passions.

OṀ ANDHAKĀSURA SŪDANĀYA NAMAḤ

Praise the Lord who killed the asura Andhaka.

OṀ GAṄGĀDHARĀYA NAMAḤ

Hail to the God who supports the river Ganges in His hair.

OṀ LALĀṬĀKṢĀYA NAMAḤ

To the Lord whose sport is creation, prostrations!

OṀ KĀLAKĀLĀYA NAMAḤ

Praise Śiva, who is the Death of death.

OṀ KṚPĀNIDHAYE NAMAḤ

To the God who is the Treasure of compassion, prostrations!

OṀ BHĪMĀYA NAMAḤ

Hail to Śiva, whose strength is awesome.

OṀ PARAŚU HASTĀYA NAMAḤ

Praise the God who wields an axe in His hands.

OṀ MṚGAPĀṆAYE NAMAḤ

To the Lord who looks after the soul in the wilderness, Hail!

OṀ JAṬĀDHARĀYA NAMAḤ

Hail to Śiva, who bears a mass of matted hair.

OṀ KAILĀSAVĀSINE NAMAḤ

Praise the great God who abides on Mt. Kailas.

OṀ KAVACINE NAMAḤ

To the Lord who is wrapped in armor, prostrations!

OṀ KAṬHORĀYA NAMAḤ

Hail to Śiva, who causes all growth.

OṀ TRIPURĀNTAKĀYA NAMAḤ

Praise the Lord who destroyed the three demonic cities.

OṀ VṚṢANKĀYA NAMAḤ

To the God whose emblem is a bull, prostrations!

OṀ VṚṢABHĀRŪḌHĀYA NAMAḤ

Hail toŚiva, who rides a bull.

OṀ BHASMODDHŪLITA VIGRAHĀYA NAMAḤ

Praise the Lord covered with holy ash.

OṀ SĀMAPRIYĀYA NAMAḤ

To the God exceedingly fond of hymns from the Sama Veda, prostrations!

OṀ SVARAMAYĀYA NAMAḤ

Hail to Śiva, who creates through sound.

OṀ TRAYĪMŪRTAYE NAMAḤ
Praise the Lord who is worshipped in three forms.

OṀ ANĪŚVARĀYA NAMAḤ
To the undisputed Lord, prostrations!

OṀ SARVAJÑĀYA NAMAḤ
Hail to the God, who knows all things.

OṀ PARAMĀTMANE NAMAḤ
Praise to the Supreme Self.

OṀ SOMASŪRĀGNI LOCANĀYA NAMAḤ
To the light in the eyes of Soma, Surya, and Agni.

OṀ HAVIṢE NAMAḤ
Hail to Śiva, who receives oblations of ghee.

OṀ YAJÑAMAYĀYA NAMAḤ
Praise to the Architect of all sacrificial rites.

OṀ SOMĀYA NAMAḤ
To the Moon-glow of the mystic's vision, prostrations!

OṀ PAṆCAVAKTRĀYA NAMAḤ
Hail to the God of the five activities.

OṀ SADĀŚIVĀYA NAMAḤ
Praise the eternally auspicious benevolent Śiva.

OṀ VIŚVEŚVARĀYA NAMAḤ
To the all-pervading Ruler of the cosmos, prostrations!

OṀ VĪRABHADRĀYA NAMAḤ
Hail to Śiva, the foremost of heroes.

OṀ GAṆANĀTHĀYA NAMAḤ
Praise the Supreme God of the Ganas.

OṀ PRAJĀPATAYE NAMAḤ
To the Creator of all that moves and breathes, prostrations!

OṀ HIRAṆYARETASE NAMAḤ
Hail to God, who emanates golden souls.

OṀ DURDHARṢAYA NAMAḤ
Praise the unconquerable Being.

OṀ GIRĪŚĀYA NAMAḤ
To the Monarch of the holy Mountain Kailas, prostrations!

OṀ GIRIŚĀYA NAMAḤ
Hail to the Lord of the Himalayas.

OṀ ANAGHĀYA NAMAḤ
Praise Lord Śiva, who can inspire no fear.

OṀ BUJAṄGABHŪṢAṆĀYA NAMAḤ
To the Lord adorned with golden snakes, prostrations!

OṀ BHARGĀYA NAMAḤ
Hail to the foremost of rishis.

OṀ GIRIDHAṆVANE NAMAḤ
Praise the God whose weapon is a mountain.

OṀ GIRIPRIYĀYA NAMAḤ
To the Lord who is fond of mountains, prostrations!

OṀ KṚTTIVĀSASE NAMAḤ
Hail to God, who wears clothes of hide.

OṀ PURĀRĀTAYE NAMAḤ
Praise the Lord who is thoroughly at home in the wilderness.

OṀ BHAGAVATE NAMAḤ
To the Lord of prosperity, prostrations!

OṀ PRAMATHĀDHIPĀYA NAMAḤ
Hail to God, who is served by goblins.

OṀ MṚTYUÑJAYĀYA NAMAḤ
Praise the Conqueror of death.

OṀ SŪKṢMATANAVE NAMAḤ
To the subtlest of the subtle, prostrations!

OṀ JAGADVYĀPINE NAMAḤ
Hail to Śiva, who fills the whole world.

OṀ JAGADGURAVE NAMAḤ
Praise the Guru of all the worlds.

OṀ VYOMAKEŚĀYA NAMAḤ
To the God whose hair is the spreading sky above, hail!

OṀ MAHĀSENAJANAKĀYA NAMAḤ
Hail to the origin of Mahasena.

OṀ CĀRUVIKRAMĀYA NAMAḤ
Praise Śiva, the guardian of wandering pilgrims.

OṀ RUDRĀYA NAMAḤ
To the Lord who is fit to be praised, prostrations!

OṀ BHŪTAPATAYE NAMAḤ
Hail to the Source of all living creatures.

OṀ STHĀṆAVE NAMAḤ
Praise the firm and immovable Deity.

OṀ AHIRBUDHNYĀYA NAMAḤ
To the Lord who waits for the sleeping kundalini, Hail!

OṀ DIGAMBARĀYA NAMAḤ
Hail to Śiva, whose robe is the cosmos.

OṀ AṢṬAMŪRTAYE NAMAḤ
Praise the Lord who has eight forms.

OṀ ANEKĀTMANE NAMAḤ
To the God who is the One Soul in all souls, prostrations!

OṀ SĀTVIKĀYA NAMAḤ
Hail to the Lord of boundless energy.

OṀ ŚUDDHA VIGRAHĀYA NAMAḤ
Praise Him who is free of all doubt and dissension.

OṀ ŚĀŚVATĀYA NAMAḤ
To Lord Śiva, endless and eternal, prostrations!

OṀ KHAṆḌAPARAŚAVE NAMAḤ
Hail to God, who cuts through the mind's despair.

OṀ AJĀYA NAMAḤ
Praise the Instigator of all that occurs.

OṀ PĀPAVIMOCAKĀYA NAMAḤ
To the Lord who releases all fetters, prostrations!

OṀ MṚDĀYA NAMAḤ
Hail to the Lord who shows only mercy.

OṀ PAŚUPATAYE NAMAḤ
Praise the Ruler of all evolving souls.

OṀ DEVĀYA NAMAḤ
To God Himself, prostrations!

OṀ MAHĀDEVĀYA NAMAḤ
Hail to the Great God.

OṀ AVYAYĀYA NAMAḤ

Praise the One never subject to change.

OṀ HARAYE NAMAḤ

To Śiva, who dissolves all bondage, prostrations!

OṀ PŪṢADANTABHIDE NAMAḤ

Hail to God, who punished Pushan.

OṀ AVYAGRĀYA NAMAḤ

Praise the Lord who is steady and unwavering.

OṀ DAKṢĀDHVARAHARĀYA NAMAḤ

Hail to the Destroyer of Daksa's conceited sacrifice.

OṀ HARĀYA NAMAḤ

To the Lord who withdraws the cosmos, prostrations!

OṀ BHAGANETRABHIDE NAMAḤ

Praise God Śiva, who taught Bhaga to see more clearly.

OṀ AVYAKTĀYA NAMAḤ

To Śiva, who is subtle and unseen, prostrations!

OṀ SAHASRĀKṢĀYA NAMAḤ

Hail to the Lord of limitless forms.

OṀ SAHASRAPADE NAMAḤ

Praise the God who is standing and walking everywhere.

OṀ APAVARGAPRADĀYA NAMAḤ

To the Lord who gives and takes all things, prostrations!

OṀ ANANTĀYA NAMAḤ

Hail to the Lord who is unending.

OṀ TĀRAKĀYA NAMAḤ

Praise the Great Liberator of mankind.

OṀ PARAMEŚVARĀYA NAMAḤ

To the Supreme Lord, prostrations!

The 108 Names of Sri Rama

OṀ ŚRĪ RĀMĀYA NAMAḤ
Salutations to Sri Rama, the Giver of Happiness

OṀ RĀMABHADRĀYA NAMAḤ
...to Rama, the Auspicious One

OṀ RĀMACHANDRĀYA NAMAḤ
...to Rama who is as lustrous as the moon

OṀ ŚĀŚVATĀYA NAMAḤ
...to the ever-lasting One

OṀ RĀJIVALOCHANĀYA NAMAḤ
...to the Lotus-eyed

OṀ ŚRĪMATE NAMAḤ
...to the Abode of Lakshmi

OṀ RĀJENDRĀYA NAMAḤ
...to the King of kings

OṀ RAGHUPUNGAVĀYA NAMAḤ
...to the Most Exalted of the Raghu dynasty

OṀ JĀNAKĪ VALLABHĀYA NAMAḤ
...to the Beloved of Janaki

OṀ JAITRĀYA NAMAḤ
...to the Triumphant

OṀ JITĀMITRĀYA NAMAḤ
...to the Conqueror of His enemies

OṀ JANĀRDHANĀYA NAMAḤ
...to the Refuge of the people

OṀ VIŚVĀMITRA PRIYĀYA NAMAḤ
...to the Beloved of Sage Vishvamitra

OṀ DĀNTĀYA NAMAḤ
...to the well-controlled One

OṀ ŚARAṆATRĀṆA TATPARĀYA NAMAḤ
...to the One who is keen to protect those who take refuge in Him

OṀ BĀLI PRAMATHANĀYA NAMAḤ
...to the Vanquisher of Bali

OṀ VĀGMINE NAMAḤ
...to the Eloquent

OṀ SATYAVĀCHE NAMAḤ
...to the One of truthful speech

OṀ SATYAVIKRAMĀYA NAMAḤ
...to the One who is valiant in defending Truth

OṀ SATYAVRATĀYA NAMAḤ
...to the One of truthful vows

OṀ VRATADHARĀYA NAMAḤ
...to the One who faithfully keeps His vows

OṀ SADĀ HANUMADĀŚRITĀYA NAMAḤ
...to the One who is always served by Hanuman

OṀ KAUSALEYĀYA NAMAḤ
...to the Son of Kausalya

OṀ KHARADHVAMSINE NAMAḤ
...to the Annihilator of the demon Khara

OṀ VIRĀDHA VANAPAṆḌITĀYA NAMAḤ
...to the Expert in destroying the demon Viradha

OṀ VIBHĪṢAṆA PARITRĀTRE NAMAḤ
...to the Protector of Vibhishana

OṀ KŌDAṆḌA KHAṆḌANĀYA NAMAḤ
...to the One who broke the mighty bow

OṀ SAPTATALA PRABHEDRE NAMAḤ
...to the One who permeates the seven planes of existence

OṀ DAŚAGRĪVA ŚIRŌHARĀYA NAMAḤ
...to the One who cut off Ravana's heads

OṀ JĀMADAGNYA MAHĀDARPPA DALANĀYA NAMAḤ
...to the One who shattered the pride of Parasurama

OṀ TĀṬAKĀNTAKĀYA NAMAḤ
...to the Slayer of Tataka

OṀ VEDĀNTA SĀRĀYA NAMAḤ
...to the Essence of Vedanta

OṀ VEDĀTMANE NAMAḤ
...to the Self of the Vedas

OṀ BHAVARŌGASYA BHEṢAJĀYA NAMAḤ
...to the Healer of the disease of Becoming

OṀ DŪṢAṆATRI ŚIRŌHANTRE NAMAḤ
...to the One who cut off the head of Dushana

OṀ TRIMŪRTAYE NAMAḤ
...to the Embodiment of the Three Gods

OṀ TRIGUṆĀTMAKĀYA NAMAḤ
...to the Source of the three gunas

OṀ TRIVIKRAMĀYA NAMAḤ
...to the Lord as Vamana

OṀ TRILŌKĀTMANE NAMAḤ
...to the Source of the Three Worlds

OṀ PUṆYACHĀRITRA KĪRTANĀYA NAMAḤ
...to the One whose story is a source of merit to those who sing it

OṀ TRILŌKA RAKṢAKĀYA NAMAḤ
...to the Protector of the Three Worlds

OṀ DHANVINE NAMAḤ
...to the Wielder of the bow

OṀ DAṆḌAKĀRAṆYA KARTANĀYA NAMAḤ
...to the Dweller in the Dandaka forest

OṀ AHALYĀ ŚĀPAŚAMANĀYA NAMAḤ
...to the Remover of Ahalya's curse

OṀ PITRU BHAKTĀYA NAMAḤ
...to the Worshipper of His father Dasaratha

OṀ VARA PRADĀYA NAMAḤ
...to the Giver of boons

OṀ JITENDRIYĀYA NAMAḤ
...to the Conqueror of the senses

OṀ JITAKRŌDHĀYA NAMAḤ
...to the Conqueror of anger

OṀ JITĀMITRĀYA NAMAḤ
...to the One who wins over friends

OṀ JAGAD GURAVE NAMAḤ
...to the Guru of the world

OṀ ṚKṢA VĀNARA SAṄGHĀTINE NAMAḤ

...to the Lord who organized the hordes of monkeys

OṀ CHITRAKŪṬA SAMĀŚRAYĀYA NAMAḤ

...to the Lord who took refuge at Chitrakuta Hill

OṀ JAYANTA TRĀṆA VARADĀYA NAMAḤ

...to the Lord who blessed Jayanta

OṀ SUMITRĀ PUTRA SEVITĀYA NAMAḤ

...to the Lord who is served by Sumitra's son (Lakshmana)

OṀ SARVA DEVĀDHI DEVĀYA NAMAḤ

...to the Lord of all the gods

OṀ MṚTAVĀNARA JĪVANĀYA NAMAḤ

...to the Lord who revived the dead monkeys (after the war)

OṀ MĀYĀMĀRĪCHA HANTRE NAMAḤ

...to the Destroyer of the demon Maricha who practiced illusion

OṀ MAHĀDEVĀYA NAMAḤ

...to the Great Lord

OṀ MAHĀBHŪJĀYA NAMAḤ

...to the Lord of mighty arms

OṀ SARVADEVA STUTĀYA NAMAḤ

...to the Lord who is praised by all the gods

OṀ SAUMYĀYA NAMAḤ

...to the Calm One

OṀ BRAHMANYĀYA NAMAḤ

...to the Absolute Reality

OṀ MUNI SAMSTUTĀYA NAMAḤ

...to the Lord who is praised by sages

OṀ MAHĀYŌGINE NAMAḤ

...to the Great Yogin

OṀ MAHĀDĀRĀYA NAMAḤ

...to the Noble One

OṀ SUGRĪVEPSITA RĀJYADAYE NAMAḤ

...to the Lord who returned the kingdom to Sugriva

OṀ SARVA PUṆYĀDHI KAPHALĀYA NAMAḤ

...to the Giver of the fruits of good karmas

OṀ SMṚTA SARVĀGHA NĀŚANĀYA NAMAḤ
...to the Remover of all afflictions

OṀ ĀDIPURUṢĀYA NAMAḤ
...to the Primal Being

OṀ PARAMAPURUṢĀYA NAMAḤ
...to the Supreme Being

OṀ MAHĀPURUṢĀYA NAMAḤ
...to the Great Being

OṀ PUṆYŌDAYĀYA NAMAḤ
...to the Source of all blessings

OṀ DAYĀSĀRĀYA NAMAḤ
...to the Embodiment of Compassion

OṀ PURĀṆA PURUṢŌTTAMĀYA NAMAḤ
...to the Most Ancient Person

OṀ SMITA VAKTRĀYA NAMAḤ
...to the One who smiling speaks

OṀ MITA BHĀṢIṆE NAMAḤ
...to the One of moderate speech

OṀ PŪRVA BHĀṢIṆE NAMAḤ
...to the One who rarely speaks

OṀ RĀGHAVĀYA NAMAḤ
...to the scion of the Raghu dynasty

OṀ ANANTA GUṆAGAMBHĪRĀYA NAMAḤ
...to the Lord of infinite majestic qualities

OṀ DHĪRŌDĀTTA GUṆŌTTAMĀYA NAMAḤ
...to the Lord of valorous qualities

OṀ MĀYĀ MĀNUṢA CHARITRĀYA NAMAḤ
...to the Lord who incarnated as a man through His Maya

OṀ MAHĀDEVĀDI PŪJITĀYA NAMAḤ
...to the Lord who is worshipped by Lord Shiva

OṀ SETUKṚTE NAMAḤ
...to the Builder of the bridge

OṀ JITA VĀRĀŚAYE NAMAḤ
...to the Conqueror of desires

OṀ SARVA TĪRTHAMAYĀYA NAMAḤ
...to the Lord who is the sum of all holy places

OṀ HARAYE NAMAḤ
...to the Destroyer

OṀ ŚYĀMĀṄGĀYA NAMAḤ
...to the Dark-complexioned One

OṀ SUNDARĀYA NAMAḤ
...to the Beautiful One

OṀ SURĀYA NAMAḤ
...to the Lord

OṀ PĪTAVĀSASE NAMAḤ
...to the Lord clad in yellow raiment

OṀ DHANURDHARĀYA NAMAḤ
...to the Bearer of the bow

OṀ SARVA YAJÑĀDHIPĀYA NAMAḤ
...to the Lord of sacrifice

OṀ YAJVINE NAMAḤ
...to the Sacrificer

OṀ JARĀMARAṆA VARJITĀYA NAMAḤ
...to the Conqueror of birth and death

OṀ VIBHĪṢAṆA PRATIṢṬHĀTRE NAMAḤ
...to the Lord who established Vibhishana on the throne

OṀ SARVĀBHARAṆA VARJITĀYA NAMAḤ
...to the Lord who relinquished all adornment

OṀ PARAMĀTMANE NAMAḤ
...to the Supreme Self

OṀ PARABRAHMAṆE NAMAḤ
...to the Supreme Absolute

OṀ SACHIDĀNANDA VIGRAHĀYA NAMAḤ
...to the Embodiment of Existence, Awareness and Bliss

OṀ PARASMAI JYOTIṢE NAMAḤ
...to the Supreme Light

OṀ PARASMAI DHĀMNE NAMAḤ
...to the Supreme Abode

OṀ PARĀKĀŚĀYA NAMAḤ
...to the Supreme Space

OṀ PARĀTPARĀYA NAMAḤ
...to the Supreme beyond the Highest

OṀ PAREŚĀYA NAMAḤ
...to the Supreme Lord

OṀ PĀRAKĀYA NAMAḤ
...to the Lord who takes His devotees across (the Ocean of Samsara)

OṀ PARĀYA NAMAḤ
...to the Supreme Being

OṀ SARVA DEVĀTMAKĀYA NAMAḤ
...to the Lord who is the Source of all gods

OṀ PARASMAI NAMAḤ
...to the Supreme Lord

Pronunciation Guide

VOWELS

A	-as	***u***	in b***u***t
Ā	-as	***a***	in f***a***r but held twice as long as **a**
AI	-as	***ai***	in ***ai***sle
AU	-as	***ow***	in h***ow***
i	-as	***i***	in p***i***n
Ī	-as	***ee***	in m***ee***t but held twice as long as **i**
Ō	-as	***o***	in g***o***al
Ṛ	-as	***ri***	in ***ri***m
U	-as	***u***	in p***u***sh
Ū	-as	***oo***	in f***oo***l

CONSONANTS

K	-as	***k***	in ***k***ite
KH	-as	***kh***	in Ec***kh***art
G	-as	***g***	in ***g***ive
GH	-as	***gh***	in di***g-h***ard
Ṅ	-as	***n***	in si***n***g
P	-as	***p***	in ***p***ine
PH	-as	***ph***	in u***p-h***ill
B	-as	***b***	in ***b***ird
BH	-as	***bh***	in ru***b-h***ard
M	-as	***m***	in ***m***other

Ṁ -a resonant nasal sound like the ***n*** in the French word bo***n***

Ḥ -coupled with a vowel, aḥ is pronounced like ***aha***, iḥ is like ***ihi***

T & Ṭ	-as	***t***	in ***t***ub
TH & ṬH	-as	***th***	in ligh***th***ouse
D & Ḍ	-as	***d***	in ***d***ove
DH & ḌH	-as	***dh***	in re***d-h***ot
Ṇ	-as	***n***	in ***n***aught

The letters with dots under them are pronounced with the tip of the tongue against the roof of the mouth, others with the tongue against the teeth

C	-as	***ch***	in ***ch***air
CH	-as	***ch***	in staun***ch-h***eart
J	-as	***j***	in ***j***oy
JH	-as	***dge***	in he***dge***hog
Ñ	-as	***ny***	in ca***ny***on
Ṣ	-as	***sh***	in ***sh***ine
Ś	-as	***s***	in the German ***s***prechen
S	-as	***s***	in ***s***un

Book Catalog

By Author

Sri Mata Amritanandamayi Devi

108 Quotes On Faith
108 Quotes On Love
Compassion, The Only Way To Peace: Paris Speech
Cultivating Strength And Vitality
Living In Harmony
May Peace And Happiness Prevail: Barcelona Speech
May Your Hearts Blossom: Chicago Speech
Practice Spiritual Values And Save The World: Delhi Speech
The Awakening Of Universal Motherhood: Geneva Speech
The Eternal Truth
The Infinite Potential Of Women: Jaipur Speech
Understanding And Collaboration Between Religions
Unity Is Peace: Interfaith Speech

Swami Amritaswarupananda Puri

Ammachi: A Biography
Awaken Children, Volumes 1-9
From Amma's Heart
Mother Of Sweet Bliss
The Color Of Rainbow

Swami Jnanamritananda Puri

Eternal Wisdom, Volumes 1-2

Swami Paramatmananda Puri

Dust Of Her Feet
On The Road To Freedom Volumes 1-2
Talks, Volumes 1-6

Swami Purnamritananda Puri

Unforgettable Memories

Swami Ramakrishnananda Puri

Eye Of Wisdom
Racing Along The Razor's Edge
Secret Of Inner Peace
The Blessed Life
The Timeless Path
Ultimate Success

Swamini Krishnamrita Prana

Love Is The Answer
Sacred Journey
The Fragrance Of Pure Love
Torrential Love

M.A. Center Publications

1,000 Names Commentary
Archana Book (Large)
Archana Book (Small)
Being With Amma
Bhagavad Gita
Bhajanamritam, Volumes 1-6
Embracing The World
For My Children
Immortal Light
Lead Us To Purity
Lead Us To The Light
Man And Nature
My First Darshan
Puja: The Process Of Ritualistic Worship
Sri Lalitha Trishati Stotram

Amma's Websites

AMRITAPURI—Amma's Home Page
Teachings, Activities, Ashram Life, eServices, Yatra, Blogs and News
http://www.amritapuri.org

AMMA (Mata Amritanandamayi)
About Amma, Meeting Amma, Global Charities, Groups and Activities and Teachings
http://www.amma.org

EMBRACING THE WORLD®
Basic Needs, Emergencies, Environment, Research and News
http://www.embracingtheworld.org

AMRITA UNIVERSITY
About, Admissions, Campuses, Academics, Research, Global and News
http://www.amrita.edu

THE AMMA SHOP—Embracing the World® Books & Gifts Shop
Blog, Books, Complete Body, Home & Gifts, Jewelry, Music and Worship
http://www.theammashop.org

IAM—Integrated Amrita Meditation Technique®
Meditation Taught Free of Charge to the Public, Students, Prisoners and Military
http://www.amma.org/groups/north-america/projects/iam-meditation-classes

AMRITA PUJA
Types and Benefits of Pujas, Brahmasthanam Temple, Astrology Readings, Ordering Pujas
http://www.amritapuja.org

GREENFRIENDS
Growing Plants, Building Sustainable Environments, Education and Community Building
http://www.amma.org/groups/north-america/projects/green-friends

FACEBOOK
This is the Official Facebook Page to Connect with Amma
https://www.facebook.com/MataAmritanandamayi

DONATION PAGE
Please Help Support Amma's Charities Here:
http://www.amma.org/donations